LA CUCINA ITALIANA

LA CUCINA ITALIANA

Consulting Editor
Gabriella Rossi

HERMES
HOUSE

First published in 1998 by Hermes House
27 West 20th Street, New York, NY 10011

HERMES HOUSE books are available for bulk purchase for sales promotion and for
premium use. For details, write or call the sales director, Hermes House, 27 West
20th Street, New York, NY 10011; (800) 354-9657

ISBN 1 84038 076 4

Publisher: Joanna Lorenz
Project Editor: Alison Macfarlane
Editor: Ruth Baldwin
Designer: Brian Weldon
Recipes: Carla Capalbo, Jacqueline Clarke, Frances Cleary, Roz Denny,
Joanna Farrow, Sarah Gates, Shirley Gill, Christine Ingram, Norma MacMillan,
Elizabeth Martin, Kate Whitman, Jeni Wright
Photographers: Karl Adamson, Steve Baxter, Michelle Garrett, Amanda Heywood,
Patrick McLeavey, Michael Michaels

Printed in Hong Kong

1 3 5 7 9 10 8 6 4 2

Contents

INTRODUCTION

Italian cooking is strongly regional—the dishes of Florence, Venice, Genoa, Piedmont, Rome and Naples all have their own character. This is largely because Italy was not unified until 1861, and although the regions are now more able (and willing) to share their natural produce, they still rely heavily on what they can grow themselves. Sun-ripened tomatoes, eggplants and peppers feature strongly in the cuisine of the south, fish is the staple food on the coast, Parmesan cheese is at its best in Parma, dairy products are used in much of the cuisine of the north (with, for example, butter replacing olive oil in many of the dishes) and the best beef is reared in Tuscany. Each area has its "classic" dish—Milan has its creamy risotto, Bologna its tagliatelle with meat sauce, Naples its pizza and Rome its lamb cooked with anchovies and herbs.

Despite the diversity of Italian cooking, the one unifying factor is the freshness of the ingredients. Produce is bought daily, sometimes even twice daily, at the local market. Dishes are often very simple—meats and fish are grilled or roasted, sauces often take no longer than the pasta to cook and delicious pizzas can be created in minutes—allowing the quality of the ingredients to do the work.

Olive oil plays a vital role in Italian cooking, and is used in nearly every recipe, from a simple salad tossed with extra virgin olive oil vinaigrette to a classic tomato sauce for pasta or the warm and crusty bread served with every meal. It is rich in monounsaturated fat and, like the low-fat carbohydrates provided by the pasta, rice and vegetables that are the base of so many dishes, contributes to the healthy diet prevalent in Italy.

Italians love their food and they love sharing it with friends and family. They take time in its preparation and time in its eating. All the delicious and authentic recipes in this book will help to capture the Italian enthusiasm for food, whether you choose to serve a simple salad or an elaborate meal.

The Italian Meal

One of the many attractions of the Italian meal is the relaxed way in which it is eaten and enjoyed. Most meals in Italy start with a plate of antipasti, particularly if pasta is not being served as a course. It could simply contain a selection of delicious olives, but will more usually include a variety of cold roasted or marinated vegetables, cold meats such as prosciutto or Parma ham, and delicious breads such as ciabatta and focaccia to mop up the juices. It could also include some hot crostini—rounds of toasted bread topped with melted cheese and various garnishes—or mini pizzas. Whatever the choice, a good quality olive oil is of the utmost importance.

Salads
Salads also feature in antipasti, but apart from the basic green salad, most can, by varying the portions, be served at any meal, as an appetizer, a side dish or even as a main course.

Soups
Soups are popular in Italy, although they are not usually eaten at the same meal as rice or pasta, as they often contain these ingredients. When soup is served as a separate course, however, it is in hearty portions. The most substantial soups are served as a main course as a light alternative to the main meal of the day.

Vegetables
Vegetables rarely accompany meat, chicken or game; a few potatoes and a green salad are considered plenty after a first course of pasta or rice. Instead, vegetables are usually eaten as a separate dish, either in small quantities as a first course, or in larger quantities as a main course. Many—green beans, artichoke hearts, peppers—are also popular ingredients in Italian salads.

Pasta and rice
Pasta, eaten in southern Italy, and rice, eaten in the north, are both traditionally served after the antipasto as a first course before the main course of fish or meat. But pasta and rice dishes can be eaten as any part of a meal and at any time of day.

Polenta
Polenta, another Italian staple, is normally eaten with a main course to soak up the juices or added to hearty dishes baked in the oven.

Cheese
Cheese, if it is eaten at all at a meal, is served after the main course. It is usually a small selection and is sometimes accompanied by a sweet pear or a ripe peach. It is also added to pizzas and some sauces, while grated Parmesan is frequently served with pasta dishes.

Desserts
Although Italians love sweets, everyday meals are normally concluded with fresh fruit. You are much more likely to see Italians eating cakes and pastries with a cup of coffee in the morning or afternoon. Elaborate desserts are kept for special occasions, often bought rather than made, and sensibly left to the skilled hands of the pastry cook.

Right: *In Italy it is the freshness of the vegetables, often bought at market on the day they are used, that makes the food so delicious.*

Equipment

Many of the utensils in the Italian kitchen are everyday items found in most kitchens, but some specialized ones are particularly useful. Pasta can be made by hand, but a pasta machine will make it much lighter work, and trying to serve spaghetti from the pan without a special spoon is very frustrating. If you are making pizzas, a cutting wheel will cut them into clean slices.

Colander
Indispensable for draining hot pasta and vegetables.

Cookie cutters
Usually used for cutting cookie dough into fancy shapes but equally good for cutting fresh pasta shapes.

Earthenware pot
Excellent for slow-cooking stews, soups or sauces. It can be used either in the oven or on top of the stove over low heat with a metal heat diffuser under it to prevent cracking. Many shapes and sizes are available. To season a terra-cotta pot before using it for the first time, immerse it in cold water overnight. Remove from the water and rub the unglazed bottom with a garlic clove. Fill with water and bring slowly to a boil. Discard the water. Repeat the process, changing the water, until the "earth" taste disappears.

Fluted pastry cutter
For cutting fresh pasta or pastry.

Hand food mill
Excellent for soups, sauces and tomato passata, the pulp passes through the holes, leaving the seeds and skin behind.

Ice cream scoop
Ideal for serving firm and well-frozen ice creams.

Italian ice cream scoop
Good for soft ices that are not too solid.

Meat mallet
Good for pounding cutlets. It can also be used to crush nuts and whole spices.

Mortar and pestle
For hand-grinding spices, coarse salt, pepper, herbs and bread crumbs.

Olive pitter
Can be used to pit olives or cherries.

Parmesan cheese knife
In Italy Parmesan is not cut with a conventional knife, but broken off the large cheese wheels using this kind of wedge. Insert the point and apply pressure.

Pasta machine
Many models are available, including sophisticated electric and industrial models. Most have an adjustable roller width and thin and wide noodle cutters.

Pasta rolling pin
A length of dowel 2 inches in diameter can also be used. Smooth the surface with fine sandpaper, rinse and dry before using for the first time.

Piping tips
For piping decorations, garnishes, etc. Use with a nylon or paper pastry bag.

Pizza cutting wheel
Useful for cutting slices, although a sharp knife may also be used.

Spaghetti spoon
The wooden "teeth" catch the spaghetti strands as they boil.

Spatula
Very useful for spreading and smoothing.

Whisk
Excellent for smoothing sauces and beating egg whites.

Wide vegetable peeler
Very easy to use for peeling all sizes of vegetable.

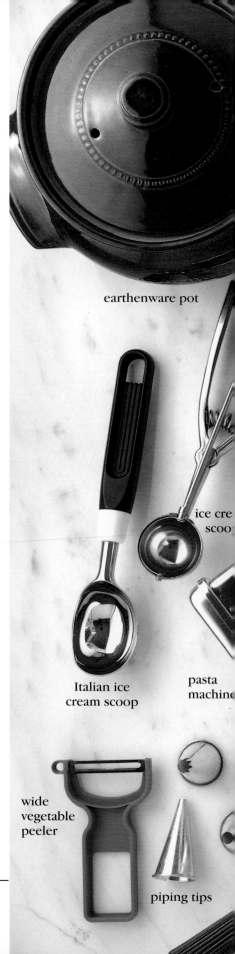

earthenware pot

ice cream scoop

Italian ice cream scoop

pasta machine

wide vegetable peeler

piping tips

mortar and
pestle

pasta
rolling pin

olive pitter

whisk

fluted
pastry
cutter

hand food mill

cookie
cutters

meat
mallet

colander

spaghetti spoon

Parmesan
cheese
knife

pizza cutting
wheel

spatula

Basic Ingredients

Cured Meats

Cured meats are a popular ingredient of antipasti, and each region has its own specialties. A typical antipasto could consist of a plate of mixed prepared meats and sausages. Salamis, pancetta, air-dried bresaola, coppa and mortadella sausages are some of the meats most commonly used in Italy, often served with crusty bread and butter. Prosciutto crudo—raw prosciutto—is the most prized of all meats, and is delicious served thinly sliced with ripe melon or fresh figs.

Cheeses

An Italian meal is more likely to end with a selection of cheeses and fruit than a sweet dessert. Among the huge variety of cheeses, the following are some of the best known:

Gorgonzola
This creamy blue cheese is made in Lombardy. It has a mild flavor when young, which becomes stronger with maturity.

Mascarpone
This is a rich, triple-cream cheese with a mild flavor. It is often used in desserts as a substitute for whipped cream.

Mozzarella
Mozzarella is a fresh, white cheese made from water buffalo's or, more commonly, cow's milk. The texture is soft and chewy and the taste mild.

Parmesan
Parmesan is a long-aged, full-flavored cheese with a hard rind, used for both grating and eating in slivers. The wheels are aged for between 18 and 36 months. Fresh Parmesan is superb, and is incomparably better than the ready-grated varieties sold pre-packed in jars.

Pecorino
There are two main types of Pecorino: Pecorino romano and Pecorino Toscano, both made from sheep's milk. This salted, sharp-flavored cheese is widely used for dessert eating, and for grating when mature.

Scamorza
A distinctively shaped cheese made from cow's milk. Its shape is the result of being hung from a string during aging.

Gorgonzola

Scamorza

Parmesan cheese

Parma ham

bresaola

mozzarella

pecorino

mortadella

cacciatoro

salami

pancetta

Pantry Ingredients

The following ingredients are all commonly used to give Italian dishes their characteristic flavors. They are good basics to keep in your pantry for use when you need them.

Amaretti cookies
Usually served with sweet wine, for dipping.

Authentic Balsamic vinegar
This has only recently become widely available outside Italy. Aged slowly in wooden barrels, the finest varieties are deliciously mellow and fragrant.

Capers
Aromatic buds pickled in jars of wine vinegar. They go well with garlic and lemon.

Dried beans
A typical Italian pantry will always contain a supply of dried natural ingredients. Dried beans and lentils should be stored in airtight containers for use in soups and stews.

Dried red chilies
Good for adding spicy flavor to all kinds of dishes.

Fennel seeds
These have a great affinity with fish, pork and poultry and can also be sprinkled on bread.

Juniper berries
These have a sweet, resinous flavor that goes well with hearty meat dishes.

Olive oil
Perhaps the single most important ingredient in a modern Italian kitchen is olive oil. The fruity flavor of a fine extra virgin olive oil perfumes any dish it is used in, from pesto sauce to the simplest salad dressing. Buy the best olive oil you can afford; one bottle goes a long way and makes a huge difference to any recipe.

Olives
These are one of Italy's most wonderful native ingredients. Unfortunately, fresh cured olives do not travel well, and many of the most delicious varieties are not available outside the Mediterranean. Sample canned or bottled olives before adding to sauces, as they sometimes acquire an unpleasant metallic taste that could spoil the flavor of the dish. Good-quality olives can be bought at the fresh food counters of supermarkets and delicatessens.

Pine nuts
These are very popular in the Mediterranean region and are an essential ingredient in pesto sauce. They have a delicate flavor and can be used in sweet and savory dishes.

Polenta
The coarsely ground yellow cornmeal is a staple of the northern Italian diet. Once cooked, it can be eaten hot or left to cool and set, then sliced and brushed with oil before broiling.

Porcini mushrooms
These mushrooms are found in the woods in various parts of Europe in autumn. They can be eaten cooked fresh, or sliced thinly and dried in the sun or in special ovens. A few dried porcini soaked in water add a deliciously woodsy flavor.

Rice
Another popular ingredient in northern Italy is rice, which is used to make risotto. Of the special varieties grown in the area for this purpose, the best known are arborio, vialone nano and carnaroli.

Sun-dried tomatoes
Packed in oil, they can be used straight from the jar in salads, sauces and stuffings.

white peppercorns

polenta

juniper berries

fennel seeds

green olives

bay leaves

salt cod

sun-dried
tomatoes

olive oil

garlic

authentic
balsamic vinegar

dried red chilies

arborio rice

green lentils

chickpeas

porcini
mushrooms

Great Northern
beans

pinto beans

capers

amaretti cookies

pine nuts

coffee beans

Fresh Produce

Italian cooking is based on the creative use of fresh, seasonal ingredients. Vegetables and herbs play central roles in almost every aspect of the menu. In the markets, there is a sense of anticipation at the beginning of each new season, heralded by the arrival, on the beautifully displayed stalls, of the year's first artichokes, olives, chestnuts or wild mushrooms. Seasonal recipes are always popular and make the most of available produce.

Regional differences

The cuisine of the hot south is typically Mediterranean: Vegetables feature in pasta dishes, on their own or in salads. In the cooler north, meat dishes are more plentiful, and there is a vast array of dairy products. Central Italy combines the best of both north and south. The one thing that all the regions have in common is that they take the best, freshest ingredients and cook them very simply. Italian cuisine is not a complicated or sophisticated style of cooking.

Vegetables

Many of the vegetables once considered exotically Mediterranean are now readily available in the markets and supermarkets of most countries. Fennel and eggplant, bell peppers, zucchini and radicchio are now increasingly present in pasta sauces, soups and pizzas, and they add a wonderful accent to meat and fish dishes too.

Wherever you shop, look for the freshest possible fruits and vegetables. Choose unblemished, firm, sun-ripened produce, preferably locally or organically grown.

Herbs

Many herbs grow freely in the Mediterranean climate, especially basil, parsley, thyme, marjoram, oregano, sage and rosemary, and they are used extensively in Italian cooking.

Fresh herbs such as basil, parsley and sage are easy to cultivate in window boxes and gardens and have an infinitely finer flavor than their dried counterparts.

If buying and using dried herbs, store them in a cool, dark place and don't keep them for too long, or they will become stale and musty.

Right, clockwise from top left: *Garlic cloves, artichokes, red onions, purple cauliflower, fennel, radicchio, fresh herbs (basil, thyme, parsley and sage), eggplants and green bell peppers.*

BASIC RECIPES

Basic Pasta Dough

Allow 1¾ cups all-purpose flour, a pinch of salt and 1 tablespoon olive oil to 2 eggs, lightly beaten, for 3–4 servings, depending on the required size of the portions.

1 Sift the flour and pinch of salt onto a clean work surface and make a well in the center with your fist.

2 Pour the beaten eggs and oil into the well. Gradually mix the eggs and oil into the flour with your fingers.

3 Knead the pasta until smooth, wrap and allow to rest for at least 30 minutes before attempting to roll out. The pasta will be much more elastic after resting.

Using a Food Processor

1 As an alternative to mixing the dough by hand as above, use a food processor. Sift the flour into the bowl and add a pinch of salt.

2 Pour in the beaten eggs and oil and chosen flavoring, if using, and process until the dough begins to come together. Remove the dough and knead until smooth. Wrap the dough and let rest for 30 minutes. Use as required.

Using a Pasta Machine

1 Feed the rested dough several times through the highest setting first, then reduce the settings until the required thickness is achieved.

2 A special cutter will produce fettuccine or tagliatelle. A narrower cutter will produce spaghetti or tagliarini.

Basic Pizza Dough

This simple bread dough is rolled out thinly for a traditional pizza recipe.

Makes one of the following:
10–12-inch round pizza crust
four 5-inch round pizza crusts
12 x 7-inch oblong pizza crust

INGREDIENTS
1½ cups white bread flour
¼ teaspoon salt
1 teaspoon rapid-rise dry yeast
½–⅔ cup lukewarm water
1 tablespoon olive oil

dry yeast

white bread flour

olive oil

1 Sift the flour and salt into a large mixing bowl.

2 Stir in the yeast.

3 Make a well in the center of the dry ingredients. Pour in the water and oil and mix with a spoon to a soft dough.

4 Knead the dough on a lightly floured surface for about 10 minutes, until smooth and elastic.

5 Place the dough in a greased bowl and cover with plastic wrap. Let sit in a warm place to rise for about 1 hour or until the dough has doubled in size.

6 Punch down the dough. Transfer to a lightly floured surface and knead again for 2–3 minutes. Roll out as required and place on a greased baking sheet. Push up the edge to make a rim. The dough is now ready for topping.

Basic Tomato Sauce for Pizza

Tomato sauce forms the basis of the topping in many pizza recipes. Make sure it is well seasoned and thick before spreading it over the crust. It will keep fresh in a covered container in the refrigerator for up to 3 days.

Covers one 10–12-inch round or 12 x 7-inch oblong pizza crust

INGREDIENTS
1 tablespoon olive oil
1 medium onion, finely chopped
1 garlic clove, finely chopped
1 can (14 ounces) chopped tomatoes
1 tablespoon tomato paste
1 tablespoon chopped fresh mixed herbs, such as parsley, thyme, basil and oregano
pinch of sugar
salt and ground black pepper

1 Heat the oil in a medium saucepan, add the onion and garlic and gently fry for about 5 minutes or until softened.

2 Add the tomatoes, tomato paste, herbs, sugar and seasoning.

3 Simmer, uncovered, stirring occasionally, for 15–20 minutes or until the tomatoes have reduced to a thick pulp. Let cool.

Basic Tomato Sauce for Pasta

Tomato sauce is without a doubt the most popular topping for pasta in Italy. This sauce is best made with fresh tomatoes of any variety, but also works well with canned plum tomatoes.

Serves 4

INGREDIENTS
¼ cup olive oil
1 medium onion, very finely chopped
1 garlic clove, finely chopped
1 pound tomatoes, fresh or canned, chopped, with their juice
salt and ground black pepper
a few fresh basil leaves or parsley sprigs

1 Heat the oil in a medium saucepan. Add the onion and cook, stirring occasionally, over medium heat for 5–8 minutes or until it is translucent.

2 Stir in the garlic, fresh tomatoes and 3 tablespoons water. If using canned tomatoes, add them with their juice instead of water and break them up with a wooden spoon. Season with salt and pepper and add the herbs. Cook for 20–30 minutes.

3 Pass the sauce through a food mill or purée in a food processor. To serve, reheat gently, adjust the seasoning, if necessary, and pour the sauce over the drained pasta.

Bolognese Meat Sauce

This great meat sauce is a specialty of Bologna. It is delicious with tagliatelle or short pasta such as penne or conchiglie, as well as spaghetti, and is indispensable in baked lasagne.

Serves 6

INGREDIENTS
2 tablespoons butter
¼ cup olive oil
1 medium onion, finely chopped
2 tablespoons finely chopped
    pancetta or unsmoked bacon
1 carrot, finely sliced
1 celery stalk, finely sliced
1 garlic clove, finely chopped
12 ounces lean ground beef
⅔ cup dry red wine
½ cup milk
1 can (14 ounces) plum
    tomatoes, chopped, with juice
1 bay leaf
¼ teaspoon fresh thyme leaves
salt and ground black pepper

butter *olive oil* *onion*

pancetta *carrot* *celery*

garlic

ground beef *milk* *red wine* *canned tomatoes*

bay leaf *thyme*

COOK'S TIP
This sauce keeps well in the refrigerator for several days and can also be frozen.

1 Heat the butter and oil in a heavy saucepan. Add the onion and cook gently for 3–4 minutes. Add the pancetta and cook until the onion is translucent. Stir in the carrot, celery and garlic. Cook for 3–4 minutes, until the vegetables are softened.

2 Add the beef and crumble it into the vegetables with a fork. Stir until the meat loses its red color. Season with salt and pepper. Pour in the wine, raise the heat slightly and cook for 3–4 minutes, until the liquid evaporates. Add the milk and cook until it evaporates.

3 Stir in the tomatoes with their juice and the herbs. Bring the sauce to a boil. Reduce the heat to low and simmer, uncovered, for 1½–2 hours, stirring occasionally. Adjust the seasoning, if necessary, and remove the bay leaf before serving.

Chopping herbs

Use this method to chop herbs until they are as coarse or as fine as desired.

1 Strip the leaves from the stalk and pile them on a cutting board.

2 Using a sharp knife, cut the herbs into small pieces, holding the tip of the blade against the board and rocking the blade back and forth.

Pasta and Chickpea Soup

A thick soup from central Italy. The addition of a sprig of fresh rosemary provides a typically Mediterranean flavor.

Serves 4–6

INGREDIENTS
1 cup dried chickpeas
3 garlic cloves, peeled
1 bay leaf
6 tablespoons olive oil
2 ounces (¼ cup) diced salt pork, pancetta or bacon
1 sprig fresh rosemary
5 ounces tiny pasta shells
salt and ground black pepper
freshly grated Parmesan cheese, to serve (optional)

garlic

chickpeas

Parmesan cheese

olive oil

bay leaf

rosemary

pancetta

tiny pasta shells

COOK'S TIP
Let the soup stand for about 10 minutes before serving. This will allow the flavor and texture to develop.

1 Soak the chickpeas in water overnight. Rinse well and drain. Place the chickpeas in a large saucepan with water to cover. Bring to a boil and boil for 15 minutes. Rinse and drain.

2 Return the chickpeas to the pan. Add water to cover, one of the garlic cloves, the bay leaf, 3 tablespoons of the oil and a pinch of pepper.

3 Simmer for about 2 hours, until tender, adding more water as necessary. Remove the bay leaf. Pass about half the chickpeas through a food mill or purée in a food processor with a few tablespoons of the cooking liquid. Return the purée to the pan with the rest of the peas and the remaining cooking water.

4 In a frying pan, sauté the diced pork gently in the remaining oil with the rosemary and remaining garlic cloves until just golden. Discard the rosemary and garlic.

5 Stir the pork with its oil into the chickpea mixture.

6 Add 2½ cups of water to the chickpea mixture, and bring to a boil. Season with salt and more pepper, if necessary. Stir in the pasta and cook until just *al dente*. Serve with grated Parmesan on the side, if desired.

Tomato and Fresh Basil Soup

A soup for late summer, when fresh tomatoes are at their most flavorful.

Serves 4–6

INGREDIENTS
1 tablespoon olive oil
2 tablespoons butter
1 medium onion, finely chopped
2 pounds ripe plum tomatoes, roughly chopped
1 garlic clove, roughly chopped
about 3 cups chicken or vegetable broth
½ cup dry white wine
2 tablespoons sun-dried tomato paste
2 tablespoons shredded fresh basil, plus a few whole sprigs to garnish
⅔ cup heavy cream
salt and pepper

olive oil   garlic   chicken broth
butter
heavy cream   onion
white wine   basil
plum tomatoes   sun-dried tomato paste

VARIATION
The soup can also be served chilled. Pour it into a container after sieving and chill for at least 4 hours. Serve in chilled bowls.

1 Heat the oil and butter in a large saucepan over medium heat until foaming. Add the onion and cook gently for about 5 minutes, stirring frequently, until it is softened but not brown.

2 Stir in the chopped tomatoes and garlic, then add the broth, white wine and sun-dried tomato paste, with salt and pepper to taste. Bring to a boil, then lower the heat, half-cover the saucepan and simmer gently for 20 minutes, stirring occasionally to prevent the tomatoes from sticking to the bottom of the pan.

3 Purée the soup with the shredded basil in a blender or food processor, then press through a sieve into a clean pan.

4 Add the heavy cream and heat through, stirring. Do not allow the soup to approach boiling point. Check the consistency and add more broth if necessary, then adjust the seasoning. Pour into heated bowls and garnish with whole basil sprigs. Serve immediately.

Roasted Plum Tomatoes with Garlic

These are so simple to prepare, yet taste absolutely wonderful. Use a large, shallow earthenware dish that will allow the tomatoes to sear and char in a hot oven.

Serves 4

INGREDIENTS

8 plum tomatoes
12 garlic cloves
¼ cup extra virgin olive oil
3 bay leaves
salt and ground black pepper
3 tablespoons fresh oregano leaves,
    to garnish

plum tomatoes   *garlic*   *olive oil*

oregano   *bay leaves*

COOK'S TIP
Select ripe, juicy tomatoes without any blemishes to get the best flavor out of this dish.

1 Preheat the oven to 450°F. Halve the plum tomatoes, leaving a small part of the green stem intact, if possible, for decoration.

2 Select an ovenproof dish that will hold all the tomatoes snugly in a single layer. Place the tomatoes in the dish with the cut side facing upward, and push the whole, unpeeled garlic cloves between them.

3 Brush the tomatoes with the oil, add the bay leaves and sprinkle black pepper over the top.

4 Bake for about 45 minutes, until the tomatoes have softened and are sizzling in the dish. They should be charred around the edges. Season with salt and a little more black pepper, if needed. Garnish with the fresh oregano leaves and serve immediately.

VARIATION
For a sweet alternative, use red or yellow bell peppers instead of the tomatoes. Cut each pepper in half and remove all the seeds before placing, cut side up, in an ovenproof dish.

Roasted Bell Peppers in Oil

Bell peppers take on a delicious, smoky flavor when roasted in a very hot oven. The skins can easily be peeled off and the flesh stored in olive oil. This oil can then be used to add extra flavor to salad dressings.

Makes one small jar

INGREDIENTS
6 large bell peppers of
    different colors
1¾ cups olive oil

bell peppers

olive oil

COOK'S TIP
These pepper slices make very attractive presents, especially around Christmas time. You can put them in special preserving jars, available at kitchen-equipment stores. Alternatively, reuse large jam jars: First, wash them thoroughly, soaking off the labels at the same time. Sterilize all jars before use by placing them upside down in a low oven for about half an hour. While the jars are still hot, add the sliced peppers, and fill with a good olive oil. Cover immediately with the lid and glue on an attractive label.

1 Preheat the oven to 450°F. Lightly grease a large baking sheet.

2 Quarter the peppers, remove the cores and seeds, then squash them flat with the back of your hand. Lay the peppers skin side up on the baking sheet.

3 Roast the peppers in the top third of the oven for 12–15 minutes, until the skins blacken and blister.

4 Remove the peppers from the oven, cover with a clean dish towel until they are cool, then peel off the skins.

5 Slice the peppers and pack them into a clean sterilized preserving jar. Add the olive oil to the jar to cover the pepper slices completely, then seal the lid tightly.

6 Store the peppers in the refrigerator and use them within 2 weeks. Use the oil in salad dressing or for cooking once the peppers have been eaten.

Artichokes with Garlic and Herb Butter

It is fun eating artichokes and even more fun to share one between two people. You can always have a second one to follow so that you get your fair share!

Serves 4

INGREDIENTS
2 large or 4 medium globe
   artichokes
salt

FOR THE GARLIC AND HERB BUTTER
6 tablespoons butter
1 garlic clove, very finely chopped
1 tablespoon chopped fresh
   mixed herbs

butter

garlic

mixed herbs

globe artichokes

1 Wash the artichokes well in cold water. Using a sharp knife, cut off the stalks level with the bases. Cut off the top ½ inch of leaves. Snip off the pointed ends of the remaining leaves with kitchen scissors and discard.

2 Put the prepared artichokes in a large saucepan of lightly salted water. Bring to a boil, cover and cook for 40–45 minutes or until one of the lower leaves comes away easily from the artichoke when gently pulled.

3 Drain upside down while making the garlic and herb butter. Melt the butter in a small saucepan over low heat, add the garlic and cook for 30 seconds. Remove from the heat, stir in the herbs and pour into one or two small serving bowls.

4 Place the artichokes on serving plates and serve immediately with the garlic and herb butter.

COOK'S TIP

To eat an artichoke, pull off each leaf and dip into the garlic and herb butter. Scrape off the soft, fleshy base with your teeth. When the center is reached, pull out the hairy choke and discard it, as it is inedible. The heart can be cut up and eaten with the remaining garlic butter.

Asparagus with Prosciutto

When asparagus are young and tender, you need do nothing more than trim off the ends of the spears. However, larger spears, with ends that are tough and woody, require some further preparation before cooking.

Serves 4

INGREDIENTS

1½–2 pounds medium asparagus
    spears
¾ cup (1½ sticks) butter, clarified
    (see Cook's Tip)
2 teaspoons lemon juice
2 tablespoons finely chopped
    scallions
1 tablespoon finely chopped fresh
    parsley
4 slices prosciutto
salt and ground black pepper

clarified butter

parsley

prosciutto

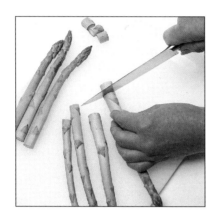

1 Cut off the tough, woody ends of the asparagus and trim the spears so that they are all about the same length.

2 If desired, remove the skin: Lay a spear flat and hold it just below the tip. With a vegetable peeler, shave off the skin, working lengthwise down the spear to the end of the stalk. Roll the spear over so that you can remove the skin from all sides.

3 Half-fill a large frying pan with salted water. Bring to a boil, add the asparagus and simmer for 4–5 minutes, or until it is just tender. (Pierce a spear to test.) Remove and drain.

4 Combine the clarified butter, lemon juice, scallions and parsley in a small saucepan. Season with salt and pepper to taste. Heat the herb butter until it is just lukewarm.

5 Divide the asparagus among four warmed plates. Drape a slice of prosciutto over each portion. Spoon the herb butter over the top and serve.

COOK'S TIP
To clarify butter, heat until it stops bubbling. Remove from the heat and let stand until the sediment has sunk to the bottom. Gently pour off the clear fat on top and strain it through cheesecloth.

asparagus   *lemon juice*   *scallions*

Insalata Tricolore

This can be a simple first course if served on individual salad plates, or as part of a mixed dish of appetizers laid out on a platter. When lightly salted, tomatoes make their own flavorful dressing with their natural juices.

Serves 4–6

INGREDIENTS
1 small red onion, thinly sliced
6 large full-flavored tomatoes
extra virgin olive oil, for sprinkling
1 small bunch arugula or watercress, roughly chopped
6 ounces mozzarella cheese, thinly sliced or grated
2 tablespoons pine nuts (optional)
salt and ground black pepper

large tomatoes   *extra virgin olive oil*

pine nuts   *small red onion*

mozzarella cheese   *arugula*

1 Soak the onion slices in a bowl of cold water for 30 minutes, then drain and pat dry. Skin the tomatoes by slashing them with a sharp knife and dipping briefly in a pan of boiling water.

2 Slice the tomatoes and divide half the slices among small plates, or arrange them on a large platter, if you prefer.

3 Sprinkle liberally with olive oil, then layer with half the chopped arugula and onion slices, seasoning well. Add half the cheese, sprinkling on more oil and seasoning as you go.

4 Repeat with the remaining tomato slices, chopped arugula, the onion slices and the cheese, adding more oil and seasoning.

5 Season well to finish and complete with some oil and a good sprinkling of pine nuts, if using. Cover the salad and chill for at least 2 hours before serving.

VARIATION
Instead of the fresh arugula or watercress, use chopped fresh basil, which goes particularly well with the flavor of ripe tomatoes.

Mixed Seafood Salad

Versions of this salad appear all along Italy's coasts. Use fresh seafood in season or a combination of fresh and frozen.

Serves 6–8

INGREDIENTS
12 ounces small squid
1 small onion, cut into quarters
1 bay leaf
8 ounces uncooked medium
   shrimp, in their shells
1½ pounds fresh mussels, in
   their shells
1 pound fresh small clams
¾ cup dry white wine
1 fennel bulb

FOR THE DRESSING
5 tablespoons extra virgin olive oil
3 tablespoons lemon juice
1 garlic clove, finely chopped
salt and ground black pepper

clams   extra virgin
              olive oil
fennel   garlic
onion   white wine
shrimp
lemon
              squid
mussels   bay leaf

1 Working near the sink, clean the squid. Peel off the thin skin from the body section. Rinse well. Pull the head and tentacles away from the body section. Some of the intestines will come away with the head. Remove and discard the translucent quill and any remaining insides from the body.

2 Cut off the tentacles and remove the small beak from the base. Discard the head and intestines. Rinse the body and tentacles under cold running water. Bring a large pan of water to a boil. Add the onion, bay leaf and squid and cook for 10 minutes, until tender. Remove with a slotted spoon, cool, then slice the body into rings ½ inch wide. Cut each tentacle in half. Set aside.

3 Drop the shrimp into the same boiling water used for the squid and cook for about 2 minutes, or until they turn pink. Remove with a slotted spoon. Peel and devein. (The cooking liquid may be strained and kept for soup.) Cut off the "beards" from the mussels. Scrub and rinse the mussels and clams well in several changes of cold water.

4 Put the mussels and clams in a large saucepan with the wine. Cover and steam for about 5 minutes, until the shells open (discard any that do not). Remove the opened shellfish with a slotted spoon.

5 Shell the clams and the mussels. Chop the fennel top and reserve for the dressing. Chop the bulb into bite-size pieces and put in a bowl with the clams, mussels, squid and shrimp.

6 Make the dressing by mixing the oil, lemon juice, garlic and chopped fennel top in a bowl. Add salt and pepper to taste. Pour onto the salad and toss well. Serve immediately.

Baked Onions with Sun-Dried Tomatoes

This wonderfully simple vegetable dish of baked onions brings together the flavors of a hot Italian summer—tomatoes, fresh herbs and olive oil.

Serves 4

INGREDIENTS
1 pound small onions, peeled
2 teaspoons chopped fresh rosemary
    or 1 teaspoon dried rosemary
2 garlic cloves, chopped
1 tablespoon chopped fresh parsley
½ cup sun-dried tomatoes in oil,
    drained and chopped
6 tablespoons olive oil
1 tablespoon white wine vinegar
salt and ground black pepper

olive oil

garlic

rosemary

small onions

sun-dried tomatoes

white wine vinegar

parsley

1 Preheat the oven to 300°F. Grease a shallow baking dish. Drop the onions into a saucepan of boiling water and cook for 5 minutes. Drain in a colander.

2 Spread the onions in the bottom of the prepared baking dish.

VARIATIONS

Other herbs can be used instead of the rosemary and parsley in this dish. Try using shredded fresh basil, which will enhance the flavor of the sun-dried tomatoes, or fresh thyme, which complements the flavor of baked onions perfectly. If you can find small red onions, these would make a nice change, or even mix the two colors.

3 Combine the rosemary, garlic, parsley, salt and pepper in a small mixing bowl and sprinkle the mixture evenly over the onions in the dish.

4 Sprinkle the chopped sun-dried tomatoes over the onions. Drizzle the olive oil and vinegar on top.

5 Cover the dish with a sheet of foil and bake for 45 minutes, basting occasionally. Remove the foil and bake for about 15 minutes more, until the onions are golden brown all over. Serve immediately from the dish.

Broiled Eggplant Bundles

These are delicious little bundles of tomatoes, mozzarella cheese and fragrant fresh basil, wrapped in slices of eggplant.

Serves 4

INGREDIENTS
2 large, long eggplants
8 ounces mozzarella cheese
2 plum tomatoes
16 large basil leaves
2 tablespoons olive oil
salt and ground black pepper

FOR THE DRESSING
¼ cup olive oil
1 teaspoon balsamic vinegar
1 tablespoon sun-dried tomato
    paste
1 tablespoon lemon juice

FOR THE GARNISH
2 tablespoons pine nuts, toasted
torn basil leaves

eggplant

mozzarella
cheese

basil

lemon

balsamic vinegar

sun-dried
tomato paste

plum
tomatoes

olive oil

pine nuts

1 To make the dressing, whisk together the olive oil, vinegar, sun-dried tomato paste and lemon juice. Season to taste and set aside.

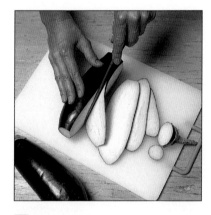

2 Remove the stalks from the eggplants and cut the eggplants lengthwise into thin slices—the aim is to get 16 slices total (each about ¼ inch thick), disregarding the first and last slices. (If you have a mandoline, it will cut perfect, even slices for you; otherwise use a sharp, long-bladed knife.)

3 Bring a large pan of salted water to a boil and cook the eggplant slices for about 2 minutes, or until just softened. Drain the sliced eggplant, then dry on paper towels. Set aside.

4 Cut the cheese into thin slices. Cut each tomato into eight slices, not counting the first and last slices.

5 Take two eggplant slices and place on a baking sheet or in a large flameproof dish, forming a cross. Place a slice of tomato in the center of the cross, season with salt and pepper, then add a basil leaf, followed by a slice of cheese, another basil leaf, a slice of tomato and more seasoning.

6 Fold the ends of the eggplant slices around the cheese and tomato filling to make a neat bundle. Repeat with the rest of the assembled ingredients to make eight bundles. Chill the bundles for about 20 minutes.

7 Preheat the broiler. Brush the bundles with olive oil and cook for about 5 minutes on each side, or until golden. Serve hot, with the dressing, and sprinkled with pine nuts and basil.

Zucchini with Onion and Garlic

Use a good-quality olive oil and sunflower oil. The olive oil gives the dish a delicious fragrance without overpowering the zucchini.

Serves 4

INGREDIENTS
1 tablespoon olive oil
1 tablespoon sunflower oil
1 large onion, chopped
1 garlic clove, finely chopped
6–7 small zucchini, cut into
    ½-inch slices
⅔ cup chicken or vegetable broth
½ teaspoon chopped fresh oregano
salt and ground black pepper
chopped fresh parsley, to garnish

garlic

zucchini

olive oil

chicken broth

sunflower oil

oregano   *onion*   *parsley*

1 Heat the olive and sunflower oils together in a large frying pan and add the chopped onion and garlic. Fry over medium heat for 5–6 minutes, until the onion has softened and is beginning to brown.

2 Add the zucchini slices and fry for about 4 minutes, until they just begin to be flecked with brown, stirring frequently.

3 Stir in the broth, oregano and seasoning and simmer gently for 8–10 minutes, or until the liquid has almost evaporated.

4 Spoon the zucchini into a warmed serving dish, sprinkle with chopped parsley and serve.

COOK'S TIP

Zucchini are very popular in Italy, grown in many kitchen gardens. They make a lovely summer dish, and take very little time to prepare. If you can find them, choose small zucchini, which tend to be much sweeter than the larger ones.

Stuffed Bell Peppers

Sweet bell peppers can be stuffed and baked with many different fillings, from leftover cooked vegetables to rice or pasta. Blanching the peppers first helps to make them tender.

Serves 6

INGREDIENTS

6 medium to large bell peppers,
  any color
1 cup raw rice
¼ cup olive oil
1 large onion, finely chopped
3 canned anchovy fillets, chopped
2 garlic cloves, finely chopped
3 medium tomatoes, peeled and cut
  into small dice
¼ cup dry white wine
3 tablespoons finely chopped fresh
  parsley
4 ounces (½ cup) mozzarella cheese,
  cut into small dice
6 tablespoons freshly grated
  Parmesan cheese
salt and pepper
Basic Tomato Sauce for Pasta (see
  Basic Recipes), to serve

bell peppers

rice

olive oil

anchovy fillets

white wine

tomato sauce

onion

garlic

mozzarella cheese

Parmesan cheese

parsley

tomatoes

Choose peppers with sturdy, even bases, so that they will stand on end unsupported in the baking dish. This will make them easier to cook and serve.

COOK'S TIP

Choose peppers with sturdy, even bases, so that they will stand on end unsupported in the baking dish. This will make them easier to cook and serve.

1 Cut the tops off the peppers. Scoop out the seeds and core. Blanch the peppers in a large pan of boiling water for 3–4 minutes. Remove and stand upside down on a rack to drain.

2 Cook the rice according to the instructions on the package, but drain and rinse it in cold water 3 minutes before the recommended cooking time has elapsed. Drain again.

3 In a large frying pan, heat 2 tablespoons of the oil and sauté the onion until soft but not brown. Stir in the anchovy pieces and the garlic and mash them. Add the tomatoes and the wine and cook for 5 minutes.

4 Preheat the oven to 375°F. Remove the tomato mixture from the heat. Stir in the rice, parsley, mozzarella and ¼ cup of the Parmesan cheese. Season the mixture with salt and pepper.

5 Pat the insides of the peppers dry with paper towels. Sprinkle with salt and pepper. Stuff the peppers with the tomato and rice mixture. Sprinkle the tops with the remaining Parmesan and the remaining oil.

6 Arrange the peppers in a shallow baking dish. Pour in enough water to come ½ inch up the sides of the peppers. Bake for 25 minutes. Serve immediately, with tomato sauce if desired. These peppers are also good served at room temperature.

Radicchio and Belgian Endive Gratin

Radicchio and Belgian endive take on a different flavor when cooked in this way. The creamy sauce combines wonderfully with the bitter leaves.

Serves 4

INGREDIENTS
2 heads radicchio
2 heads Belgian endive
½ cup sun-dried tomatoes in oil,
    drained and roughly chopped,
    oil reserved
salt and ground black pepper

FOR THE SAUCE
2 tablespoons butter
2 tablespoons all-purpose flour
1 cup milk
pinch of grated nutmeg
2 ounces (½ cup) grated Emmenthal
    cheese
chopped fresh parsley,
    to garnish

radicchio

Emmenthal cheese

butter

Belgian endive

sun-dried tomatoes

flour

milk

nutmeg

parsley

1 Preheat the oven to 350°F. Grease a 5-cup baking dish. Trim the radicchio and Belgian endive and discard any damaged or wilted leaves. Quarter them lengthwise and arrange in the baking dish. Sprinkle the sun-dried tomatoes on top and brush the leaves liberally with oil from the sun-dried tomato jar. Sprinkle with salt and pepper and cover with foil. Bake for 15 minutes, then remove the foil and bake for another 10 minutes, until the vegetables are softened.

COOK'S TIP

In Italy, radicchio and Belgian endive are often grilled on an outdoor barbecue. To do this, simply prepare the vegetables as above and brush with olive oil. Place cut side down on the grill for 7–10 minutes, until browned. Turn and grill for about 5 more minutes, or until the other side is browned.

2 Make the béchamel sauce. Place the butter in a small saucepan and melt over medium heat. When the butter is foaming, add the flour and cook for 1 minute, stirring. Remove from the heat and gradually add the milk, whisking constantly. Return to the heat, bring to a boil and simmer for 2–3 minutes, until the mixture thickens.

3 Season the sauce to taste and add the grated nutmeg.

4 Pour the sauce over the vegetables and sprinkle with the grated cheese. Bake for 20 minutes, or until golden brown. Serve immediately, garnished with the chopped parsley.

Tuscan Baked Beans

Beans, both dried and fresh, are particularly popular in Tuscany, where they are cooked in many different ways. In this vegetarian dish, the beans are flavored with fresh sage leaves.

Serves 6–8

INGREDIENTS
1 pound, 6 ounces dried beans,
    such as Great Northern
¼ cup olive oil
2 garlic cloves, crushed
3 fresh sage leaves
1 leek, finely sliced
1 can (14 ounces) plum tomatoes,
    chopped, with their juice
salt and ground black pepper

Great Northern beans

olive oil

canned tomatoes

garlic

leek

sage

COOK'S TIP
If fresh sage is unavailable, use ¼ cup chopped fresh parsley instead.

1 Carefully pick over the beans, discarding any stones or other particles. Place the beans in a large bowl and cover with water. Let soak for at least 6 hours or overnight. Drain.

2 Preheat the oven to 350°F. In a small saucepan, heat the oil and sauté the garlic cloves and sage leaves for 3–4 minutes. Remove from the heat and set aside.

3 In a large, deep baking dish, combine the beans with the leek and tomatoes. Stir in the oil with the garlic and sage. Add enough fresh water to cover the beans by 1 inch. Mix well. Cover the dish with a lid or foil and place in the center of the oven. Bake for 1¾ hours.

4 Remove the dish from the oven, stir the beans and season with salt and pepper. Return the beans to the oven, uncovered, and cook for another 15 minutes, or until the beans are tender. Remove from the oven and let stand for 7–8 minutes before serving. Alternatively, let cool and serve at room temperature.

Malfatti with Red Sauce

If you ever felt dumplings were a little heavy, try these light spinach and ricotta malfatti instead. Serve with a tomato and red bell pepper sauce.

Serves 4–6

INGREDIENTS

1 pound fresh leaf spinach,
 stems trimmed
1 small onion, chopped
1 garlic clove, finely chopped
1 tablespoon olive oil
14 ounces (1¾ cups) ricotta cheese
3 eggs, beaten
2 tablespoons butter, melted
1 cup dried bread crumbs
½ cup all-purpose flour
1 teaspoon salt
½ cup freshly grated Parmesan
 cheese, plus shavings to garnish
grated nutmeg, to taste
salt and ground black pepper

FOR THE SAUCE

1 large red bell pepper, seeded and
 chopped
1 small red onion, chopped
2 tablespoons olive oil
1 can (14 ounces) chopped tomatoes
⅔ cup water
generous pinch of dried oregano
2 tablespoons light cream

spinach onion ricotta cheese
garlic olive oil bread crumbs flour eggs
nutmeg Parmesan cheese light cream canned tomatoes red bell pepper butter dried oregano red onion

1 Blanch the spinach in the tiniest amount of water until it is limp. Drain well, pressing it in a sieve with the back of a ladle or spoon. Chop finely.

2 Lightly fry the onion and garlic in the oil in a large frying pan for 5 minutes. Allow to cool, then mix in the spinach, ricotta, eggs, melted butter, bread crumbs, flour, 1 teaspoon salt, grated Parmesan and grated nutmeg to taste.

3 Mold the spinach mixture into 12 small quenelles (see Cook's Tip).

4 Meanwhile, make the sauce. Lightly sauté the red pepper and onion in the oil in a saucepan for 5 minutes. Add the canned tomatoes, water, oregano and seasoning. Bring to a boil, then simmer gently for 5 minutes.

5 Remove the sauce from the heat and blend to a purée in a food processor. Return to the pan, then stir in the cream. Adjust the seasoning if necessary.

COOK'S TIP

Quenelles are oval-shaped dumplings. To shape the malfatti into quenelles you need two teaspoons. Scoop up the mixture with one spoon, making sure that it is mounded up, then, using the other spoon, scoop the mixture off the first spoon, twisting the top spoon into the bowl of the second. Repeat this action two or three times until the quenelle is nice and smooth, and then gently transfer it to a plate ready to cook. Repeat the process with the rest of the mixture.

6 Bring a shallow pan of salted water to a gentle boil, drop the malfatti into it a few at a time and poach them for about 5 minutes. Drain them well and keep them warm in a low oven.

7 Arrange the malfatti on warm plates and drizzle with the sauce. Serve topped with shavings of Parmesan.

Tomato Risotto

Creamy risotto is a classic Italian dish that can be made with a wide variety of ingredients, from a few simple herbs to mushrooms and seafood. Here, plum tomatoes provide a fresh, vibrant flavor and meaty texture.

Serves 4

INGREDIENTS

1 ½ pounds firm ripe tomatoes, preferably plum
4 tablespoons butter
1 onion, finely chopped
about 5 cups vegetable broth
1 ½ cups raw arborio rice
1 can (14 ounces) cannellini beans, drained
2 ounces (½ cup) Parmesan cheese, finely grated
salt and ground black pepper
10–12 basil leaves, shredded, and freshly grated Parmesan cheese, to serve

plum tomatoes

Parmesan cheese

vegetable broth

butter

basil *onion*

canned cannellini beans *arborio rice*

1 Preheat the broiler. Halve the tomatoes and scoop out the seeds into a sieve placed over a bowl. Press the seeds with a spoon to extract the juice. Set aside.

2 Arrange the tomatoes on a broiling pan skin side up and broil until the skins are blackened and blistered. Let sit for a while until they are cool enough to handle. Gently rub off the tomato skins using your hands and discard. Dice the flesh into even-size pieces.

3 Melt the butter in a large frying pan, add the onion and cook for 5 minutes, until beginning to soften. Add the tomatoes, the reserved juice and seasoning, then cook the mixture, stirring occasionally, for about 10 minutes. Meanwhile, bring the vegetable broth to a boil in a saucepan.

4 Add the rice to the tomato mixture and stir to coat. Add a ladleful of the broth and simmer, stirring gently, until it is absorbed. Repeat, adding a ladleful of broth at a time, until all the broth is absorbed and the rice is tender and creamy.

5 Stir in the cannellini beans and finely grated Parmesan and gently heat through for a few minutes.

6 Just before serving the risotto, sprinkle each portion with shredded basil leaves and freshly grated Parmesan.

Polenta with Mushrooms

This dish is delicious made with a mixture of wild and regular button mushrooms.

Serves 6

INGREDIENTS

2 tablespoons dried porcini
    mushrooms (omit if using
    wild mushrooms)
¼ cup olive oil
1 small onion, finely chopped
1½ pounds mushrooms, wild
    or button, or a combination
    of both
2 garlic cloves, finely chopped
3 tablespoons chopped fresh parsley
3 medium tomatoes, peeled
    and diced
1 tablespoon tomato paste
¾ cup warm water
¼ teaspoon fresh thyme leaves,
    or 1 large pinch dried thyme
1 bay leaf
2½ cups polenta or yellow cornmeal
salt and ground black pepper
fresh parsley sprigs, to garnish

1 Soak the dried mushrooms, if using, in a small bowl of warm water for about 20 minutes. Remove the mushrooms with a slotted spoon. Filter the soaking water through a layer of paper towels placed in a sieve and reserve. Rinse the mushrooms well in several changes of cold water.

2 In a large frying pan, heat the oil and sauté the onion over low heat until soft and golden.

3 Clean the fresh mushrooms by wiping them with a damp cloth. Cut into slices. When the onion is soft, add the mushrooms to the pan. Stir over medium to high heat until they release their liquid. Add the garlic, parsley and diced tomatoes. Cook for 4–5 minutes.

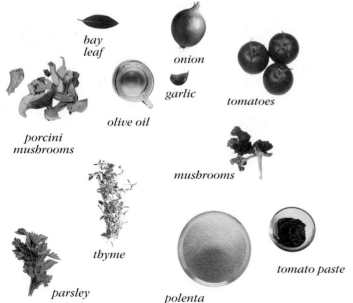

bay
leaf

onion

garlic

tomatoes

olive oil

porcini
mushrooms

mushrooms

thyme

tomato paste

parsley

polenta

4 Soften the tomato paste in the warm water (use only ½ cup water if using dried mushrooms). Add the paste mixture to the pan with the herbs. Add the dried mushrooms and soaking liquid, if using, and season. Reduce the heat to low and cook for 15–20 minutes. Set aside.

5 Bring 6¼ cups water to a boil in a large, heavy saucepan. Add 1 tablespoon salt. Reduce the heat to a simmer and begin to add the polenta in a fine stream. Stir constantly with a whisk until the polenta has all been incorporated.

COOK'S TIP
Just a few dried porcini mushrooms will help give button mushrooms a more complex and interesting flavor.

6 Switch to a long-handled wooden spoon and continue to stir the polenta over low to medium heat until it is a thick mass and pulls away from the sides of the pan. This may take 25–50 minutes, depending on the type of polenta used. For best results, never stop stirring the polenta until you remove it from the heat. When the polenta has almost finished cooking, gently reheat the mushroom sauce.

7 To serve, spoon the polenta onto a warmed serving platter. Make a well in the center. Spoon some of the mushroom sauce into the well, and garnish with parsley sprigs. Serve immediately, passing the remaining sauce in a separate bowl.

Frittata with Sun-Dried Tomatoes

Adding just a few sun-dried tomatoes gives this frittata a distinctly Mediterranean flavor.

Serves 3–4

INGREDIENTS
6 sun-dried tomatoes, dry or in oil
    and drained
¼ cup olive oil
1 small onion, finely chopped
pinch of fresh thyme leaves
6 eggs
½ cup (2 ounces) freshly grated
    Parmesan cheese
salt and ground black pepper

sun-dried tomatoes

Parmesan cheese

eggs

thyme

onion

olive oil

1 Place the dry tomatoes in a small bowl and pour in enough hot water to just cover them. Soak for about 15 minutes. Lift the tomatoes out of the water, and slice them into thin strips. Reserve the soaking water.

2 Heat the oil in a large nonstick or heavy frying pan. Stir in the onion, and cook for 5–6 minutes, or until soft and golden. Add the tomatoes and thyme. Stir over medium heat for 2–3 minutes. Season with salt and pepper.

3 Break the eggs into a bowl and beat lightly. Stir in 3–4 tablespoons of the tomato soaking water and the grated Parmesan. Raise the heat under the pan.

VARIATION
Replace the sun-dried tomatoes with ⅓ cup diced ham or prosciutto and 1 cup chopped cooked spinach. When frying the onion, add a finely chopped garlic clove if desired.

4 When the oil is sizzling, pour in the eggs. Mix them quickly into the other ingredients, and stop stirring. Lower the heat to medium and cook for 4–5 minutes on the first side, or until the frittata is puffed and golden brown.

5 Take a large plate, place it upside down over the pan and, holding it firmly with oven mitts, turn the pan and the frittata over onto it. Slide the frittata back into the pan, and continue cooking until golden on the second side, 3–4 more minutes. Serve immediately.

Roast Monkfish with Garlic and Fennel

In the past monkfish was sometimes used as a substitute for lobster meat because it is very similar in texture. It is now appreciated in its own right and is delicious quickly roasted.

Serves 4

INGREDIENTS
2½ pounds monkfish tail
8 garlic cloves
1 tablespoon olive oil
2 fennel bulbs, sliced
juice and zest of 1 lemon
bay leaves
salt and ground black pepper

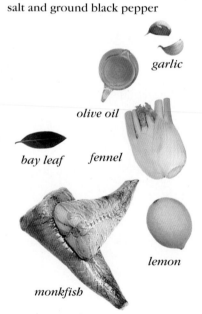

garlic

olive oil

bay leaf   *fennel*

monkfish   *lemon*

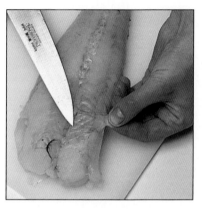

1 Preheat the oven to 425°F. With a filleting knife, cut away the thin membrane covering the outside of the monkfish.

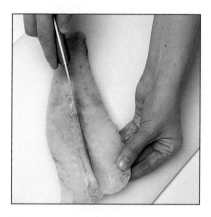

2 Cut along one side of the central bone to remove the fillet. Repeat on the other side.

3 Tie the separated fillets together with string to reshape as a tailpiece.

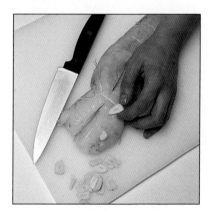

4 Peel and slice the garlic cloves and cut incisions into the monkfish flesh. Place the garlic slices into the incisions.

5 Heat the oil in a large, heavy saucepan and quickly cook the monkfish on all sides.

6 Remove the monkfish from the saucepan and place in a roasting pan together with the fennel slices, lemon juice, 1 bay leaf and seasoning. Roast for about 20 minutes, until tender and cooked through. Serve immediately, garnished with bay leaves and lemon zest.

COOK'S TIP
The anise-like flavor of fennel goes particularly well with fish. The feathery tops can be used as a garnish if desired.

Grilled Squid

If you like your food hot, chop some—or all—of the chili seeds with the flesh. If not, cut the chilies in half lengthwise, scrape out the seeds and discard them before chopping the flesh.

Serves 2

INGREDIENTS
2 whole prepared squid,
  with tentacles
5 tablespoons olive oil
2 tablespoons balsamic vinegar
¾ cup raw arborio rice
2 fresh red chilies, finely chopped
¼ cup dry white wine
salt and ground black pepper
fresh parsley sprigs, to garnish

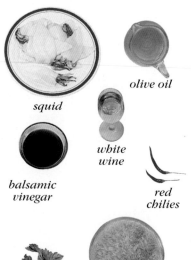

squid

olive oil

white wine

balsamic vinegar

red chilies

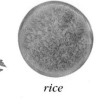

rice

parsley

1 Make a cut down the body of each squid, then open out flat. Score the flesh with the tip of a sharp knife. Chop the tentacles. Place the squid in a glass dish. Whisk oil and vinegar. Add seasoning and pour over the squid. Cover and marinate for 1 hour. Meanwhile, cook the rice in salted water until tender.

2 Heat a cast-iron grill pan. Add the body of one of the squid. Cook over medium heat for 2–3 minutes per side, pressing with a spatula. Place on a plate. Cook the other body in the same way.

3 Cut the squid bodies into diagonal strips. Pile the hot rice in the center of heated soup plates and arrange the strips of squid on top. Keep hot.

4 Put the tentacles and chilies in a heavy frying pan. Toss over medium heat for 2 minutes. Stir in the wine, then drizzle the mixture over the squid and rice. Garnish with parsley and serve.

Shrimp in Tomato Sauce

The tomato sauce base can be sharpened up by adding hot chilies.

Serves 6

INGREDIENTS

6 tablespoons olive oil
1 medium onion, finely chopped
1 celery stalk, finely chopped
1 small red bell pepper, seeded
    and chopped
½ cup dry red wine
1 tablespoon wine vinegar
1 can (14 ounces) plum tomatoes,
    chopped, with their juice
2¼ pounds uncooked medium
    shrimp, in their shells
2–3 garlic cloves, finely chopped
3 tablespoons finely chopped
    fresh parsley
1 dried red chili, crumbled or
    chopped (optional)
salt and ground black pepper

olive oil *onion* *red wine*

*red bell
pepper*

*canned plum
tomatoes*

celery

wine vinegar

garlic

shrimp *parsley*

*dried red
chili*

1 In a heavy saucepan, heat half the oil. Add the onion and cook over low heat until soft. Stir in the celery and bell pepper and cook for 5 minutes. Raise the heat and add the wine, vinegar and tomatoes. Bring to a boil and cook for 5 minutes. Lower the heat, cover the pan and simmer for about 30 minutes, until the vegetables are soft.

2 Allow the mixture to cool a little, then purée through a food mill.

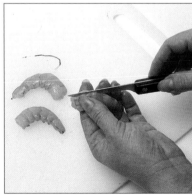

3 Shell the shrimp. Make a shallow incision with a small sharp knife down the center of the back and remove the long, black vein with the tip of a knife.

4 Heat the remaining oil in a clean, heavy saucepan. Stir in the chopped garlic and parsley, plus the chili, if using. Cook over medium heat, stirring, until the garlic is golden. Add the prepared tomato sauce and bring to a boil.

5 Stir in the shrimp. Bring the sauce back to a boil. Reduce the heat slightly and simmer until the shrimp are pink and firm: This will take 6–8 minutes, depending on their size. Season to taste and serve on warmed plates.

Pan-Fried Red Mullet with Basil and Citrus

Red mullet is popular all over the Mediterranean. This Italian recipe combines it with oranges and lemons, which grow in abundance there.

Serves 4

INGREDIENTS
4 red mullet, about
    8 ounces each, filleted
6 tablespoons olive oil
10 black peppercorns, crushed
2 oranges, 1 peeled and sliced and
    1 squeezed
1 lemon
2 tablespoons all-purpose flour
1 tablespoon butter
2 canned anchovy fillets, drained
    and chopped
¼ cup shredded fresh basil
salt and ground black pepper

basil   lemon

peppercorns   butter

flour

orange

anchovy fillets   olive oil

red mullet

COOK'S TIP
If you prefer, use other fish fillets for this dish, such as striped bass or red snapper.

1 Place the fish fillets in a shallow dish in a single layer. Pour the olive oil over them and sprinkle with the crushed peppercorns. Lay the orange slices on top of the fish. Cover the dish and let marinate in the refrigerator for at least 4 hours.

2 Halve the lemon, then remove the skin and pith from one half using a small, sharp knife and slice thinly. Squeeze the juice from the other half.

3 Lift the fish out of the marinade and pat dry with paper towels. Reserve the marinade and orange slices. Season the fish with salt and pepper and dust lightly with flour.

4 Heat 3 tablespoons of the marinade in a frying pan. Add the fish and fry for 2 minutes on each side. Remove from the pan and keep warm. Discard the marinade that is left in the pan.

5 Melt the butter in the pan with any of the remaining original marinade. Add the anchovies and cook until they are completely softened.

6 Stir in the orange and lemon juice, then check the seasoning and simmer until slightly reduced. Stir in the basil. Place the fish on a warmed serving plate, pour the sauce on top and garnish with the reserved orange slices and the lemon slices. Serve immediately.

Baked Mussels and Potatoes

This dish originated in Puglia, which is noted for its imaginative baked casseroles.

Serves 2–3

INGREDIENTS
1½ pounds large mussels, in their shells
8 ounces potatoes, unpeeled
5 tablespoons olive oil
2 garlic cloves, finely chopped
8 fresh basil leaves, torn into pieces
8 ounces tomatoes, peeled and thinly sliced
3 tablespoons dried bread crumbs
salt and ground black pepper

mussels

basil

potatoes

olive oil

garlic

bread crumbs

tomatoes

1 Cut the "beards" off the mussels. Scrub well and soak in several changes of cold water. Discard any with broken shells. Place the mussels with a cupful of water in a large saucepan, covered, over medium heat. As soon as they open, lift them out. (Discard any that do not open.) Remove and discard the empty half-shells, leaving the mussels in the other half. Strain any liquid in the pan through a layer of paper towels and reserve.

2 Boil the potatoes in salted water until they are almost cooked but still firm, then peel and slice them thinly.

3 Preheat the oven to 350°F. Spread 2 tablespoons of the olive oil in the bottom of a shallow ovenproof dish. Cover with the potato slices in one layer. Add the mussels in their half-shells in one layer. Sprinkle with garlic and pieces of basil.

4 Cover with a layer of the tomato slices. Sprinkle with bread crumbs and salt and pepper, the strained mussel liquid and the remaining olive oil. Bake for about 20 minutes, or until the tomatoes are soft and the bread crumbs are golden. Serve directly from the baking dish.

Sea Bass en Papillote

A dramatic presentation to delight your guests.
Bring the unopened packages to the table and let
them unfold their own fish to release the
delicious aroma.

Serves 4

INGREDIENTS
8 tablespoons (1 stick) butter
1 pound fresh leaf spinach
3 shallots, finely chopped
4 small sea bass, gutted
¼ cup dry white wine
bay leaves
salt and ground black pepper
new potatoes and glazed carrots,
    to serve

butter

bay leaves

white wine

spinach

shallots

sea bass

new potatoes

carrots

1 Preheat the oven to 350°F. Melt 3 tablespoons of the butter in a large, heavy saucepan, add the spinach and cook gently until almost a purée. Let cool.

2 Melt another 3 tablespoons of the butter in a clean, heavy saucepan and add the shallots. Gently sauté for 5 minutes, until the shallots are soft but not browned. Add the shallots to the spinach and let cool.

3 Season the fish both inside and outside, then stuff the insides with the spinach and shallot filling.

4 For each package, fold a large sheet of parchment or waxed paper in half and cut around the fish laid on one half to make a heart shape when unfolded. It should be at least 2 inches larger than the fish all around. Melt the remaining butter and brush a little onto the paper. Set the fish on one side of the paper.

5 Add a little wine and a bay leaf to each fish package.

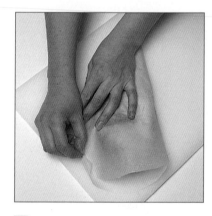

6 Fold the other side of the paper over the fish and make small pleats to seal the two edges, starting at the curve of the heart. Brush the outsides with butter. Transfer the packages to a baking sheet and bake for 20–25 minutes, until the packages are brown. Serve with new potatoes and glazed carrots.

Fresh Tuna and Tomato Stew

A deliciously simple dish that relies on good basic ingredients. For real Italian flavor, serve with polenta or pasta.

Serves 4

INGREDIENTS

12 baby onions, peeled
2 pounds ripe tomatoes
1½ pounds fresh tuna
3 tablespoons olive oil
2 garlic cloves, finely chopped
3 tablespoons chopped fresh herbs
2 bay leaves
½ teaspoon sugar
2 tablespoons sun-dried tomato paste
⅔ cup dry white wine
salt and ground black pepper
baby zucchini and fresh herbs,
    to garnish

baby onions

herbs

garlic   *bay leaves*

olive oil

tomatoes

sugar

white wine

tuna

sun-dried tomato paste   *baby zucchini*

1 Leave the onions whole and cook in a pan of boiling water for 4–5 minutes, until softened. Drain.

2 Slit the tomato skins and plunge the tomatoes into boiling water for 30 seconds. Refresh them in cold water. Peel away the skins and chop roughly.

VARIATION

Two large mackerel make a less expensive alternative to the tuna. Fillet them and cut into chunks or simply lay the whole fish over the sauce and cook, covered with a lid, until the mackerel is cooked through. Sage, rosemary and oregano all go extremely well with this dish. Choose whichever herb you prefer, or use a mixture.

3 Cut the tuna into 1-inch chunks. Heat the oil in a large frying pan and quickly fry the tuna until browned. Remove from the pan, drain and keep warm. Add the onions, garlic, tomatoes, chopped herbs, bay leaves, sugar, tomato paste and wine to the pan and bring to a boil.

4 Reduce the heat and simmer gently for 5 minutes, breaking up the tomatoes with a wooden spoon. Return the fish to the pan and cook for another 5 minutes. Remove the bay leaves, season and serve hot, garnished with baby zucchini and fresh herbs.

Stuffed Flounder Rolls

Sun-dried tomatoes, pine nuts and anchovies make a flavorful combination for the stuffing mixture.

Serves 4

INGREDIENTS

4 flounder fillets, about 8 ounces
    each, skinned
6 tablespoons butter
1 small onion, chopped
1 celery stalk, finely chopped
2 cups fresh white bread crumbs
3 tablespoons chopped fresh parsley
2 tablespoons pine nuts, toasted
3–4 pieces sun-dried tomatoes in
    oil, drained and chopped
1 can (2 ounces) anchovy fillets,
    drained and chopped
5 tablespoons fish or vegetable broth
ground black pepper

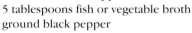

flounder   *anchovy fillets*

fish stock   *onion*

celery

butter

pine nuts   *sun-dried tomatoes*

parsley

white bread crumbs

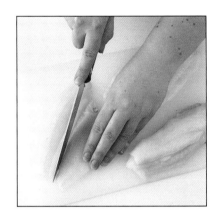

1 Preheat the oven to 350°F. Using a sharp knife, cut each fish fillet in half lengthwise to make eight smaller fillets. Melt the butter in a frying pan and add the onion and celery. Cover and cook over low heat for about 15 minutes, until softened. Do not let brown.

2 Combine the bread crumbs, parsley, pine nuts, sun-dried tomatoes and anchovies in a large bowl. Stir in the softened vegetables with the buttery juices and season with pepper to taste.

3 Divide the stuffing into eight portions. Taking one portion at a time, form the stuffing into balls, then roll up each one inside a fish fillet. Secure each roll with a toothpick.

4 Place the rolls in a buttered ovenproof dish. Pour in the stock and cover the dish with buttered foil. Bake for 20 minutes, or until the fish flakes. Remove the toothpicks. Serve the fish with some cooking juice drizzled on top.

Roast Lamb with Rosemary

In Italy lamb is traditionally served at Easter. This simple roast with potatoes owes its wonderful flavor to the fresh rosemary and garlic. It makes the perfect Sunday lunch at any time of year, served with seasonal vegetables.

Serves 4

INGREDIENTS
½ leg of lamb, 3–3½ pounds
2 garlic cloves, cut lengthwise into thin slivers
7 tablespoons olive oil
leaves from 4 sprigs fresh rosemary, finely chopped
about 1 cup lamb stock or vegetable broth
1½ pounds potatoes, cut into 1-inch cubes
a few fresh sage leaves, chopped
salt and ground black pepper
lightly cooked baby carrots, to serve

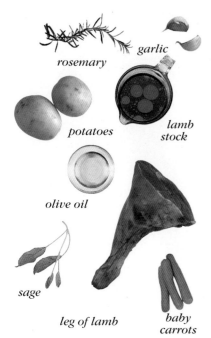

rosemary   *garlic*

potatoes   *lamb stock*

olive oil

sage

leg of lamb   *baby carrots*

1 Preheat the oven to 450°F. Using the point of a sharp knife, make deep incisions in the lamb, especially near the bone, and insert the garlic slivers into the holes.

4 Roast for another 1¼–1½ hours, until the lamb is tender, turning it two or three more times and adding the rest of the stock in two or three batches. Baste the lamb each time it is turned, to prevent the meat from drying out.

COOK'S TIP
If desired, the cooking juices can be strained and used to make a thin gravy flavored with stock and red wine.

2 Put the lamb in a roasting pan and rub it all over with 3 tablespoons of the oil. Sprinkle with about half the chopped rosemary, patting it on firmly, and season with plenty of salt and pepper. Roast for 30 minutes, turning once.

5 Meanwhile, put the potatoes in a separate roasting pan and toss with the remaining oil and rosemary and the sage. Roast, on the same oven rack as the lamb if possible, for 45 minutes, turning them several times until golden and tender.

3 Lower the oven temperature to 375°F. Turn the lamb over again and add ½ cup of the stock to the pan.

6 Transfer the lamb to a carving board, cover with a foil "tent" and let stand in a warm place for 10 minutes. Serve whole or carved into thin slices, surrounded by the potatoes and accompanied by carrots.

Beef Stew with Red Wine

This rich, hearty dish should be served with mashed potatoes or polenta.

Serves 6

INGREDIENTS

5 tablespoons olive oil
2½ pounds lean stewing beef, cut
    into 1½-inch cubes
1 medium onion, very finely sliced
2 carrots, chopped
3 tablespoons finely chopped
    fresh parsley
1 garlic clove, chopped
1 bay leaf
a few fresh thyme sprigs, or pinch
    of dried thyme
pinch of grated nutmeg
1 cup dry red wine
1 can (14 ounces) plum tomatoes,
    chopped, with their juice
½ cup beef or chicken broth
about 15 black olives, pitted
    and halved
1 large red bell pepper, seeded and
    cut into strips
salt and ground black pepper

garlic
stewing beef
nutmeg
bay leaf
onion
parsley
red wine
carrots
thyme
black olives
canned plum tomatoes
olive oil
red bell pepper
chicken broth

1 Preheat the oven to 350°F. Heat 3 tablespoons of the oil in a large, heavy, flameproof casserole. Brown the meat, a little at a time, turning it to color on all sides. Remove each batch to a plate while the remaining meat is being browned.

2 When all the meat cubes have been browned and removed, add the remaining oil, the onion and the carrots. Cook over low heat until the onion softens. Add the parsley and garlic and cook for 3–4 more minutes.

3 Return the meat to the pan, raise the heat and stir well to mix the vegetables with the meat. Stir in the bay leaf, thyme and nutmeg. Add the wine, bring to a boil and cook, stirring, for 4–5 minutes. Stir in the tomatoes, broth and olives and mix well. Season with salt and pepper. Cover the casserole and place in the middle of the oven. Bake for 1½ hours.

4 Remove the casserole from the oven. Stir in the strips of red pepper. Return the casserole to the oven and cook, uncovered, for 30 more minutes, or until the beef is tender. Serve hot.

Calf's Liver with Balsamic Vinegar

This sweet-and-sour liver dish is a specialty of Venice. Serve it very simply, with green beans sprinkled with browned bread crumbs.

Serves 2

INGREDIENTS

1 tablespoon all-purpose flour
½ teaspoon finely chopped
    fresh sage
4 thin slices calf's liver, cut into
    serving pieces
3 tablespoons olive oil
2 tablespoons butter
2 small red onions, sliced and
    separated into rings
⅔ cup dry white wine
3 tablespoons balsamic vinegar
pinch of sugar
salt and ground black pepper
fresh sage sprigs, to garnish
green beans sprinkled with
    browned bread crumbs, to serve

flour

olive oil

butter

red onions

white wine

bread crumbs

green beans

sugar

balsamic vinegar

sage

calf's liver

1 Spread out the flour in a shallow bowl. Season it with the sage and plenty of salt and pepper. Turn the liver in the flour until well coated.

2 Heat 2 tablespoons of the oil with half the butter in a wide, heavy saucepan or frying pan until foaming. Add the onion rings and cook gently, stirring frequently, for about 5 minutes, until softened but not colored. Remove with a spatula and set aside.

4 Add the wine and vinegar to the pan and stir to mix with the pan juices and any browned bits in the pan. Add the onions and sugar and heat through, stirring. Spoon the sauce over the liver, garnish with sage sprigs and serve immediately with the green beans sprinkled with bread crumbs.

3 Heat the remaining oil and butter in the pan until foaming, add the liver and cook over medium heat for 2–3 minutes on each side. Transfer to heated dinner plates and keep hot.

Chicken with Chianti

Together, the robust, full-flavored red wine and tomato pesto give this sauce a rich color and almost spicy flavor, while the grapes add a delicious sweetness. Serve the stew with grilled polenta or crusty bread, and accompany with arugula leaves for a contrasting hint of bitterness.

Serves 4

INGREDIENTS
3 tablespoons olive oil
4 bone-in chicken breast halves, skinned
1 medium red onion
2 tablespoons tomato pesto
1¼ cups Chianti
1¼ cups water
1 small bunch red grapes, halved lengthwise and seeded if necessary
salt and ground black pepper
chopped fresh parsley, to garnish
arugula leaves, to serve

chicken breasts

olive oil

Chianti

tomato pesto

red onion

parsley

arugula leaves

red grapes

COOK'S TIP
Use bone-in chicken breast halves in preference to boneless chicken for this dish, as they have a better flavor. Chicken thighs or drumsticks could also be cooked in this way.

1 Heat 2 tablespoons of the oil in a wide, heavy saucepan or large frying pan, add the chicken breasts and sauté over medium heat for about 5 minutes, until they have changed color on all sides. Remove with a slotted spoon and drain on paper towels. Cut the onion in half through the root. Trim off the root, then slice the onion halves lengthwise to create thin wedges.

2 Heat the remaining oil in the pan, add the onion wedges and pesto and cook gently, stirring constantly, for about 3 minutes, until the onion is softened but not browned.

4 Reduce the heat, then cover the pan and simmer gently for about 20 minutes, or until the chicken is tender and cooked through, stirring occasionally.

VARIATION
Use plain pesto instead of tomato, and substitute a dry white wine such as Pinot Grigio for the Chianti, then finish with seedless green grapes. A few spoonfuls of mascarpone cheese can be added at the end, if desired, to enrich the sauce.

3 Add the Chianti and water to the pan and bring to a boil, stirring, then return the chicken to the pan and add salt and pepper to taste.

5 Add the grapes to the pan and cook over low heat until heated through. Taste the sauce and adjust the seasoning if necessary. Serve the chicken hot with the arugula leaves and garnished with chopped parsley.

Polpette with Mozzarella and Tomato

These Italian meat patties are made with beef and topped with mozzarella cheese and fresh tomato.

Serves 6

INGREDIENTS
½ slice white bread, crust removed
3 tablespoons milk
1½ pounds ground beef
1 egg, beaten
⅔ cup dried bread crumbs
vegetable oil, for frying
2 beefsteak or other tomatoes, sliced
1 tablespoon chopped fresh oregano
8 ounces mozzarella cheese, cut
    into 6 slices
6 canned anchovy fillets, drained
    and cut in half lengthwise
salt and ground black pepper

bread

milk

ground beef

bread crumbs

oregano

egg

beefsteak tomatoes

vegetable oil

anchovy fillets

mozzarella cheese

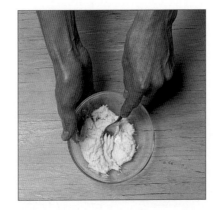

1 Preheat the oven to 400°F. Put the bread and milk into a small saucepan and heat very gently until the bread absorbs all the milk. Transfer the bread to a bowl, mash it to a pulp and let cool.

2 Put the ground beef in a bowl with the bread mixture, the egg and seasoning. Mix well, then shape the mixture into six patties. Sprinkle the bread crumbs onto a plate and dredge the patties, coating them thoroughly.

3 Heat about ¼ inch oil in a large frying pan. Add the patties and fry for 2 minutes on each side, until brown. Transfer to a greased ovenproof dish, in a single layer.

4 Lay a slice of tomato on top of each patty, sprinkle with oregano and season with salt and pepper. Place a mozzarella slice on top of each. Arrange two strips of anchovy, placed in a cross, on top of each slice of cheese.

5 Bake for 10–15 minutes, until the cheese has melted and the patties are cooked through. Serve hot, straight from the dish.

Pork Chops with Gremolata

Gremolata is a popular Italian garnish of garlic, citrus zest and parsley.

Serves 4

INGREDIENTS
2 tablespoons olive oil
4 center-cut pork chops
1 medium onion, chopped
2 garlic cloves, finely chopped
2 tablespoons tomato paste
1 can (14 ounces) chopped tomatoes
⅔ cup dry white wine
1 bouquet garni
3 canned anchovy fillets, drained and chopped
salt and ground black pepper
salad greens, to serve

FOR THE GREMOLATA
3 tablespoons chopped fresh parsley
grated zest of ½ lemon and 1 lime
1 garlic clove, chopped

onion
pork chops
garlic
tomato paste
white wine
canned tomatoes
bouquet garni
lime
anchovy fillets
parsley
lemon
olive oil
salad greens

1 Heat the oil in a large, flameproof casserole, add the pork chops and brown on both sides. Remove the chops from the casserole and set aside.

2 Add the onion to the casserole and cook until soft and beginning to brown. Add the garlic and cook for 1–2 minutes, then stir in the tomato paste, chopped tomatoes with their liquid and white wine. Add the bouquet garni. Bring to a boil, then boil rapidly for 3–4 minutes to reduce and thicken slightly.

3 Return the pork to the casserole, then cover and cook for about 30 minutes. Stir in the chopped anchovies. Cover the casserole and cook for another 15 minutes, or until the pork is tender and cooked through.

4 Meanwhile, to make the gremolata, combine the chopped fresh parsley, lemon and lime zests and garlic. Mix well and set aside.

5 Remove the pork chops and discard the bouquet garni. Reduce the sauce over high heat, if it has not already thickened. Taste the sauce and add salt and pepper as necessary.

6 Return the pork chops to the casserole, then sprinkle with the gremolata. Cover and cook for another 5 minutes. Serve hot with salad greens.

Veal with Tomatoes and White Wine (Osso Buco)

This famous Milanese dish is rich and hearty. It is traditionally served with risotto alla Milanese, but Tomato Risotto would go equally well.

Serves 4

INGREDIENTS
2 tablespoons all-purpose flour
4 veal shank crosscuts
2 small onions
2 tablespoons olive oil
1 large celery stalk, finely chopped
1 medium carrot, finely chopped
2 garlic cloves, finely chopped
1 can (14 ounces) chopped tomatoes
1¼ cups dry white wine
1¼ cups chicken broth or veal stock
1 strip of thinly pared lemon zest
2 bay leaves, plus extra for
    garnishing
salt and ground black pepper

FOR THE GREMOLATA
2 tablespoons finely chopped fresh
    flat-leaf parsley
finely grated zest of 1 lemon
1 garlic clove, finely chopped

onions   *celery*   *carrot*   *olive oil*   *canned tomatoes*

bay leaves   *garlic*   *flour*   *white wine*

chicken broth   *lemon*   *parsley*

COOK'S TIP
Veal shanks are available at large supermarkets and good butchers. Choose pieces about ¾ inch thick.

1 Preheat the oven to 325°F. Season the flour with salt and pepper and spread it out in a shallow dish. Add the veal shanks and turn them in the flour until evenly coated. Shake off any excess flour.

4 Add the chopped tomatoes with their liquid, wine, broth or stock, lemon zest and bay leaves, then season with salt and pepper. Bring to a boil, stirring.

2 Slice one of the onions into rings. Heat the oil in a large flameproof casserole, then add the veal, with the onion rings, and brown the veal on both sides over medium heat. Remove the veal with tongs and set aside to drain.

5 Return the veal shanks to the pan and coat thoroughly with the sauce. Cover and bake for 2 hours, or until the veal feels tender when pierced with a fork.

3 Chop the remaining onion and add to the pan with the celery, carrot and garlic. Stir the bottom of the pan to mix in the juices and brown bits. Cook gently, stirring frequently, for about 5 minutes, until the vegetables soften slightly.

6 Meanwhile, make the gremolata. Combine the parsley, lemon zest and garlic. Remove the casserole from the oven and discard the lemon zest and bay leaves. Taste the sauce for seasoning. Serve hot, sprinkled with the gremolata and garnished with extra bay leaves.

Garlic Chicken on a Bed of Vegetables

This is the perfect after-work dinner-party dish: It is quick to prepare and full of sunshiny flavors.

Serves 4

INGREDIENTS

4 bone-in chicken breast halves,
    2 pounds total weight
1 cup soft cheese with garlic and
    herbs (e.g. Boursin)
1 pound zucchini
2 red bell peppers, seeded
1 pound plum tomatoes
4 celery stalks
3 tablespoons olive oil
2 small onions, roughly chopped
3 garlic cloves, crushed
8 sun-dried tomatoes in oil, drained
    and roughly chopped
1 teaspoon dried oregano
2 tablespoons balsamic vinegar
1 teaspoon paprika
salt and ground black pepper
olive ciabatta or crusty bread,
    to serve

1 Preheat the oven to 375°F. Loosen the skin of each chicken breast, without removing it, to make a pocket. Divide the cheese into quarters and push one quarter underneath the skin of each chicken breast, spreading it in an even layer.

2 Cut the zucchini and bell peppers into similar-size chunks. Quarter the tomatoes and thickly slice the celery stalks.

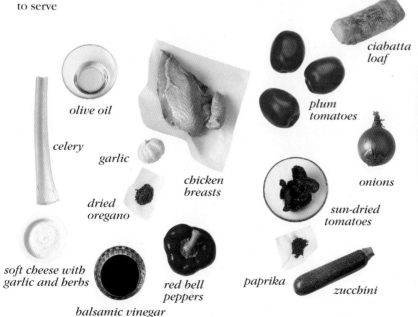

olive oil

celery

garlic

chicken breasts

dried oregano

soft cheese with garlic and herbs

balsamic vinegar

red bell peppers

paprika

zucchini

ciabatta loaf

plum tomatoes

onions

sun-dried tomatoes

3 Heat 2 tablespoons of the oil in a large, shallow, flameproof casserole. Cook the onions and garlic for 4 minutes, until the onions are soft and golden, stirring frequently.

4 Add the chopped zucchini, peppers and celery and cook for 5 more minutes.

5 Stir in the plum tomatoes, sun-dried tomatoes, oregano and balsamic vinegar. Season well with salt and pepper.

6 Place the chicken on top, drizzle with the remaining olive oil and season with salt and paprika. Bake for 35–40 minutes, or until the chicken is golden and cooked through. Serve with plenty of olive ciabatta or crusty bread.

Meat-stuffed Cabbage Rolls

Stuffed cabbage leaves are a good way of using up cooked meats and make a satisfying luncheon dish.

Serves 4–5

INGREDIENTS

1 head Savoy cabbage
4-6 slices white bread
a little milk
12 ounces lean ground beef or cold cooked meat, very finely chopped
1 egg, beaten
2 tablespoons finely chopped fresh parsley
1 garlic clove, finely chopped
½ cup freshly grated Parmesan cheese
pinch of grated nutmeg
5 tablespoons olive oil
1 medium onion, finely chopped
1 cup dry white wine
salt and ground black pepper

1 Cut the leaves from the cabbage, reserving the innermost part for a soup. Blanch the leaves, a few at a time, in a large pan of boiling water for 4–5 minutes. Refresh under cold water. Spread the leaves out on clean dish towels to dry.

2 Cut the crust from the bread and discard. Dice the bread and soak it in a little milk for about 5 minutes. Squeeze out the excess moisture with your hands.

Savoy cabbage

white wine

ground beef

milk

egg   *garlic*

onion

nutmeg

white bread

Parmesan cheese   *olive oil*

parsley

3 In a mixing bowl, combine the ground or chopped meat with the egg and soaked bread. Stir in the parsley, garlic and Parmesan cheese. Season with nutmeg, salt and pepper to taste.

4 Divide any very large cabbage leaves in half, discarding the rib. Lay the leaves out on a flat surface. Form little sausage-shaped mounds of stuffing and place them at the edge of each leaf. Roll up the leaves, tucking the ends in as you roll. Squeeze each roll lightly in the palm of your hand to help the leaves stick.

VARIATION

Serve the cabbage rolls with a tomato sauce, spooned on top just before serving.

5 In a large pan big enough to hold all the rolls in one layer, heat the olive oil. Add the onion and cook gently until it softens. Raise the heat slightly and add the rolls, turning them with a wooden spoon as they begin to cook.

6 Pour in half the wine. Cook over low to medium heat, until the wine has evaporated. Add the rest of the wine, cover the pan and cook for 10–15 more minutes. Remove the lid and cook until all the liquid has evaporated. Remove from the heat and let rest for 5 minutes before serving.

Baked Lasagne with Meat Sauce

This traditional creamy lasagne is exquisite.

Serves 8–10

INGREDIENTS
1 batch Bolognese Meat Sauce (see Basic Recipes)
14 ounces dried lasagne noodles
1 cup grated Parmesan cheese
3 tablespoons butter
salt and ground black pepper

FOR THE BÉCHAMEL SAUCE
3 cups milk
1 bay leaf
3 blades mace
8 tablespoons (1 stick) butter
⅔ cup all-purpose flour

Bolognese Meat Sauce

lasagne

Parmesan cheese

butter

all-purpose flour

milk

bay leaf

mace

1 Prepare the meat sauce. Set aside. Butter a large, shallow baking dish. Preheat the oven to 400°F. Make the sauce. Gently heat the milk with the bay leaf and mace in a saucepan. Melt the butter in a separate saucepan.

2 Add the flour to the butter and mix in well with a whisk. Cook for 2–3 minutes. Strain the hot milk into the flour and butter and mix with the whisk. Bring to a boil, stirring constantly, and cook for 4–5 minutes. Season and set aside.

3 Bring a large pot of water to a boil and add salt and half the lasagne sheets. Cook for 4 minutes less than the time recommended on the package. Cover a large work surface with a clean cloth. Remove the lasagne from the pan and drop into a bowl of cold water for 30 seconds. Remove and lay them out flat, without overlapping, on the cloth. Repeat for the second batch of lasagne.

6 Bake for 20 minutes, or until brown on top. Remove from the oven and let stand for 5 minutes before serving. Serve directly from the baking dish, cutting out rectangular or square sections for each helping.

4 To assemble the lasagne, have all the elements at hand: the baking dish, béchamel and meat sauces, pasta strips, grated Parmesan and butter. Spread one large spoonful of the meat sauce over the bottom of the dish. Arrange a layer of pasta over the meat sauce, cutting it with a sharp knife so that it fits well inside the dish.

5 Cover with a thin layer of meat sauce, then one of béchamel. Sprinkle with a little cheese. Repeat the layers in the same order, ending with a layer of pasta coated with béchamel. Do not make more than about six layers of pasta. Use the pasta trimmings to patch any gaps in the pasta. Sprinkle the top with Parmesan, and dot with butter.

COOK'S TIP

If you have any of the sauces and pasta left over, do not throw them away. Instead, use them to make a small lasagne, layering the pasta and sauce in the same way. If you wish, you can then freeze the lasagne, uncooked, to use another day.

Spaghetti with Meatballs

No Italian menu would be complete without succulent meatballs served on a bed of spaghetti. Accompany this dish with a light green salad and some warm, crusty bread.

Serves 4

INGREDIENTS
12 ounces spaghetti
salt and ground black pepper
fresh rosemary sprigs, to garnish
freshly grated Parmesan cheese,
    to serve

FOR THE MEATBALLS
1 medium onion, chopped
1 garlic clove, chopped
12 ounces ground lamb
1 egg yolk
1 tablespoon chopped fresh parsley
1 tablespoon olive oil

FOR THE SAUCE
1¼ cups passata (see Cook's Tip)
2 tablespoons chopped fresh basil
1 garlic clove, chopped

spaghetti

rosemary

basil

fresh parsley

Parmesan cheese

onion

passata

egg

garlic

olive oil

ground lamb

1 To make the meatballs, combine the onion, garlic, lamb, egg yolk, parsley and seasoning until well blended.

2 Divide the mixture into 20 pieces and mold into balls. Place on a baking sheet, cover with plastic wrap and chill for 30 minutes.

3 Heat the oil in a large frying pan and place the meatballs in it.

4 Fry the meatballs for about 10 minutes, turning occasionally, until browned on all sides. Spoon off any excess fat, without removing the meatballs.

5 For the sauce, add the passata, basil and garlic and seasoning to the pan and bring to a boil. Cover and simmer for 20 minutes, until the meatballs are tender.

COOK'S TIP

Passata is available in jars, cans or cartons at specialty Italian grocery stores and most large supermarkets. It is made from sieved tomatoes, so if you cannot find any, drain and sieve canned tomatoes instead.

The meatballs can be made a day in advance. Place them on a baking sheet, cover with plastic wrap and chill.

6 Meanwhile, bring a large pot of salted water to a boil. Add the pasta and cook according to the package instructions until it is just al dente. Drain thoroughly and divide it among four plates. Spoon on the meatballs and some of the sauce. Garnish each portion with a fresh rosemary sprig and serve immediately with plenty of freshly grated Parmesan cheese.

Pasta with Spring Vegetables

This delicious vegetarian dish is perfect for a light lunch or supper.

Serves 4

INGREDIENTS

4 ounces broccoli florets
4 ounces baby leeks
½ regular bunch asparagus
1 small fennel bulb
1 cup fresh or frozen peas
3 tablespoons butter
1 shallot, chopped
3 tablespoons chopped fresh mixed
   herbs, such as parsley, thyme
   and sage
1¼ cups heavy cream
12 ounces dried penne
salt and ground black pepper
freshly grated Parmesan cheese,
   to serve

broccoli *peas*

butter *penne*

heavy cream *Parmesan cheese*

mixed herbs

asparagus *baby leeks* *shallot*

fennel

1 Divide the broccoli florets into tiny sprigs. Cut the leeks and asparagus diagonally into 2-inch lengths. Trim the fennel bulb and remove any tough outer leaves. Cut into wedges, leaving the layers attached at the root ends so that the pieces stay intact.

2 Cook each prepared vegetable, including the peas, separately in boiling salted water until just tender—use the same water for each vegetable. Drain well and keep warm.

3 Melt the butter in a separate pan, add the chopped shallot and cook, stirring occasionally, until softened but not browned. Stir in the herbs and cream and cook for a few minutes, until slightly thickened. Meanwhile, bring a large pot of salted water to a boil.

4 Add the pasta to the boiling water and cook according to the package instructions until it is just al dente. Drain well and add to the sauce with the vegetables. Toss gently and season with plenty of pepper. Serve hot with a sprinkling of freshly grated Parmesan.

Tagliatelle with Mushrooms

The mushroom sauce is quick to make and the pasta cooks very quickly; both need to be cooked as near to serving as possible, so careful coordination is required.

Serves 4

INGREDIENTS
about 4 tablespoons butter
8–12 ounces chanterelles
1 tablespoon all-purpose flour
⅔ cup milk
6 tablespoons crème fraîche
1 tablespoon chopped fresh parsley
10 ounces fresh or dried tagliatelle
olive oil, for tossing
salt and ground black pepper

butter
flour
chanterelles
milk
crème fraîche
parsley
olive oil
tagliatelle

COOK'S TIP
Chanterelles are a little tricky to wash, as they are so delicate. However, since these are woodland mushrooms, it's important to clean them thoroughly. Hold each one by the stalk and let cold water run under the gills to dislodge hidden dirt. Shake gently to dry.

1 Melt 3 tablespoons of the butter in a frying pan and fry the mushrooms for 2–3 minutes over low heat until the juices begin to run, then increase the heat and cook until the liquid has almost evaporated. Transfer the cooked mushrooms to a bowl using a slotted spoon.

2 Stir the flour into the pan, adding a little more butter if necessary, and cook for about 1 minute, then gradually stir in the milk to make a smooth sauce.

3 Add the crème fraîche, mushrooms, parsley and seasoning and stir well. Cook very gently to heat through and then keep warm while cooking the pasta.

4 Bring a large pot of salted water to a boil. Add the pasta and cook according to the package instructions until it is just al dente. Drain well, toss with a little olive oil and then transfer to a warmed serving plate. Pour the mushroom sauce on top and serve immediately while it is hot.

VARIATION
If chanterelles are unavailable, use other wild mushrooms of your choice.

Baked Seafood Spaghetti

In this dish, each portion is baked and served in an individual package, which is then opened at the table. Use baking parchment or aluminum foil to make the packages.

Serves 4

INGREDIENTS

1 pound mussels, in their shells
½ cup dry white wine
¼ cup olive oil
2 garlic cloves, finely chopped
1 pound tomatoes, peeled and
    finely chopped
14 ounces spaghetti or other
    long pasta
8 ounces uncooked medium
    shrimp, peeled and deveined
2 tablespoons chopped fresh parsley
salt and ground black pepper

mussels   *white wine*

olive oil

tomatoes

garlic   *spaghetti*

shrimp   *parsley*

1 Scrub the mussels well under cold running water, cutting off the "beards" with a small, sharp knife. Place the mussels and the wine in a large saucepan and heat, covered, until the mussels open.

2 Lift out the mussels with a slotted spoon and set aside. (Discard any that do not open.) Strain the cooking liquid through paper towels and reserve until needed. Preheat the oven to 300°F.

3 In a medium saucepan, heat the oil and garlic together for 1–2 minutes. Add the tomatoes and cook over medium to high heat until they soften. Stir in ¾ cup of the cooking liquid from the mussels. Bring a large pot of salted water to a boil. Add the pasta and cook according to the package instructions until it is just al dente.

4 Just before draining the pasta, add the shrimp and the chopped parsley to the tomato sauce. Cook for 2 minutes, or until the shrimp are firm. Taste one and adjust the seasoning if necessary, then remove from the heat.

5 Prepare four pieces of baking parchment or foil measuring about 18 x 12 inches. Place each sheet in the center of a shallow bowl. (The bowl under the paper will prevent the sauce from spilling while the packages are being closed.) Transfer the drained pasta to a bowl. Add the tomato sauce and mix well. Stir in the mussels.

COOK'S TIP
Bottled mussels or clams may be substituted for fresh shellfish in this recipe: Add them to the tomato sauce with the shrimp. Canned tomatoes may be used instead of fresh ones.

6 Divide the pasta and seafood mixture among the four pieces of paper or foil, placing a mound in the center of each and twisting the ends together to make a closed package. Arrange on a large baking sheet and place in the middle of the oven. Bake for 8–10 minutes. Place one unopened package on each individual serving plate.

Pasta with Tomato Sauce and Roasted Vegetables

Roasting the vegetables at a high temperature concentrates their flavors wonderfully, for a sauce that almost oozes sunshine.

Serves 4

INGREDIENTS

1 eggplant
2 zucchini
1 large onion
2 red or yellow bell peppers, seeded
1 pound tomatoes
2–3 garlic cloves, coarsely chopped
¼ cup olive oil
1 cup Basic Tomato Sauce for Pasta
   (see Basic Recipes)
⅓ cup black olives, halved
   and pitted
1 pound dried pasta shapes, such as
   rigatoni or penne
3 tablespoons shredded fresh basil
salt and ground black pepper
freshly grated Parmesan cheese,
   to serve (optional)

1 Preheat the oven to 475°F. Cut the eggplant, zucchini, onion, peppers and tomatoes into 1½-inch chunks. Discard all the tomato seed.

3 Roast the vegetables for about 30 minutes, until they are soft and browned (don't worry if the edges are charred black). Stir halfway through the cooking time.

5 Bring a large pot of salted water to a boil. Add the pasta and cook according to the package instructions until it is just al dente.

6 Meanwhile, heat the tomato and roasted vegetable sauce, stirring occasionally. Taste and adjust the seasoning if necessary.

7 Drain the pasta and return it to the pan. Add the tomato and roasted vegetable sauce and mix well. Serve hot, sprinkled with the shredded basil. If desired, sprinkle with freshly grated Parmesan cheese.

zucchini

eggplant
onion
black olives

tomatoes

basil
olive oil

garlic
penne

peppers

Basic Tomato Sauce

Parmesan cheese

2 Spread out the vegetables in a large roasting pan. Sprinkle the garlic and oil over the vegetables and stir and turn to mix evenly. Season with salt and pepper.

4 Scrape the vegetable mixture into a saucepan. Add the tomato sauce and the halved olives.

Pizza Margarita

This classic pizza is simple to prepare once you have the basics on hand. The sweet flavor of sun-ripened tomatoes works wonderfully with the basil and mozzarella.

Serves 2–3

INGREDIENTS
1 pizza crust, 10–12 inches in
    diameter (see Basic Recipes)
2 tablespoons olive oil
1 batch Basic Tomato Sauce
    for Pizza (see Basic Recipes)
5 ounces mozzarella cheese
2 ripe tomatoes, thinly sliced
6–8 fresh basil leaves
2 tablespoons freshly grated
    Parmesan cheese
ground black pepper

basil

olive oil

mozzarella

tomatoes

Parmesan cheese

Basic Tomato Sauce

pizza crust

1 Preheat the oven to 425°F. Brush the pizza crust with 1 tablespoon of the oil and then spread the tomato sauce over it, leaving a small border around the edge.

2 Using a sharp knife, cut the mozzarella cheese into thin slices.

3 Arrange the sliced mozzarella and tomatoes on top of the tomato sauce on the pizza crust.

4 Roughly tear the basil leaves and sprinkle them on top of the pizza with the Parmesan cheese. Drizzle with the remaining oil and season with pepper. Bake for 15–20 minutes, until crisp and golden. Serve immediately.

Quattro Stagioni Pizza

This traditional pizza is divided into quarters, each with a different topping to depict the four seasons of the year.

Serves 2–4

INGREDIENTS
3 tablespoons olive oil
1 cup button mushrooms, sliced
1 pizza crust, 10–12 inches in
    diameter (see Basic Recipes)
1 batch Basic Tomato Sauce
    for Pizza (see Basic Recipes)
2 ounces Parma ham
6 black olives, pitted and chopped
4 bottled artichoke hearts in
    oil, drained
3 canned anchovy fillets, drained
2 ounces mozzarella cheese,
    thinly sliced
8 fresh basil leaves, shredded
ground black pepper

1 Preheat the oven to 425°F. Heat 1 tablespoon of the oil in a large frying pan and fry the mushrooms until all the juices have evaporated. Let the mushrooms cool.

2 Brush the pizza crust with half the remaining oil. Spread with the tomato sauce and score into four equal sections with a knife.

artichoke hearts

mozzarella cheese

basil

Parma ham

black olives

Basic Tomato Sauce

pizza crust

anchovy fillets

button mushrooms

olive oil

3 Arrange the mushrooms over one section of the pizza.

4 Cut the Parma ham into thin strips and arrange the strips with the olives on another section of the pizza.

5 Thinly slice the artichoke hearts and arrange on a third section. Halve the anchovies lengthwise and arrange with the mozzarella over the fourth section.

COOK'S TIP
You can use your imagination for the four toppings for this pizza. Try adding seafood such as cooked clams, mussels or shrimp for one quarter, cooked broccoli florets for another and roasted bell peppers and garlic for two others.

6 Sprinkle the basil over the pizza. Drizzle with the remaining oil and season with pepper. Bake for 15–20 minutes, until crisp and golden. Serve immediately, cut into slices.

Pepperoni Pizza

This popular pizza is spiced with green chilies and pepperoni. You can make the dish less hot by omitting some of the chilies.

Serves 2–3

INGREDIENTS

1 pizza crust, 10–12 inches in
    diameter (see Basic Recipes)
1 tablespoon olive oil
1 can (4 ounces) chopped green
    chilies, drained
1 batch Basic Tomato Sauce for
    Pizza (see Basic Recipes)
3 ounces sliced pepperoni
8–10 black olives, pitted
1 tablespoon chopped fresh oregano
1 cup grated mozzarella cheese
fresh oregano leaves, to garnish

black olives

green chilies

pepperoni

Basic Tomato Sauce

mozzarella cheese

olive oil

oregano

pizza crust

1 Preheat the oven to 425°F. Brush the pizza crust with the oil.

2 Stir the chopped green chilies into the tomato sauce, and spread the sauce over the pizza crust.

3 Arrange the sliced pepperoni on the tomato sauce on the pizza crust.

4 Halve the olives lengthwise and sprinkle them over the pepperoni with the oregano.

5 Sprinkle the grated mozzarella on top and bake for 15–20 minutes, until the pizza is crisp and golden.

6 Garnish with fresh oregano leaves and serve immediately.

VARIATION

You can make this pizza as hot as you like. For a really fiery version, use fresh red or green chiles, cut into thin slices, instead of the canned chilies.

Choux Pastries with Two Custards

Italian pastry shops are filled with displays of sweetly scented pastries such as these.

Makes about 48

INGREDIENTS
scant 1 cup water
8 tablespoons (1 stick) butter
1-inch piece vanilla bean, split
    lengthways
1¼ cups all-purpose flour
5 eggs
pinch of salt

FOR THE CUSTARD FILLINGS
2 ounces semisweet chocolate
1¼ cups milk
4 egg yolks
scant ⅓ cup granulated sugar
generous ⅓ cup all-purpose flour
1 teaspoon pure vanilla extract
1¼ cups whipping cream
unsweetened cocoa powder and
    confectioners' sugar, for dusting

butter   eggs

granulated
sugar

unsweetened
chocolate   confectioners'
sugar

water   cocoa
powder

milk

vanilla
extract

flour   whipping
cream

1 Preheat the oven to 375°F. Heat the water with the butter, vanilla bean and salt. When the butter has just melted, whisk in the flour.

2 Cook over low heat, stirring constantly, for about 8 minutes. Remove from the heat. Beat in the eggs one at a time. Remove the vanilla bean.

3 Butter a baking sheet. Spoon the mixture into a pastry bag fitted with a plain tip. Squeeze the mixture out onto the sheet into about 48 balls the size of small walnuts, leaving space between the rows to allow for spreading. Bake for 20–25 minutes, or until the pastries are golden brown. Remove from the oven and let cool thoroughly before filling.

4 Meanwhile, prepare the custard fillings. Melt the chocolate in the top half of a double boiler, or in a bowl set over a pan of simmering water. Heat the milk in a small saucepan over low to medium heat, taking care not to let it boil.

5 Beat the egg yolks with a wire whisk or electric beater. Gradually add the sugar and continue beating until the mixture is pale yellow. Beat in the flour. Add the hot milk very gradually, pouring it in through a sieve. When all the milk has been added, pour the mixture into a heavy saucepan and bring to a boil. Simmer for 5–6 minutes, stirring.

COOK'S TIP
Although the choux pastries can be made in advance, do not add the filling until the very last minute before serving, as it will make the pastry soggy and unappetizing.

6 Remove from the heat and divide the custard between two bowls. Add the melted chocolate to one and stir the vanilla extract into the other. Let cool completely.

7 Whip the cream. Fold half of it carefully into each of the custards. Fill two pastry bags fitted with plain tips with the custards. Fill half of the choux pastries with the chocolate custard, and the rest with the vanilla custard, making a little hole and piping the filling in through the side of each pastry. Dust the tops of the chocolate-filled pastries with cocoa powder, and the rest with confectioners' sugar. Serve immediately.

Fresh Orange Granita

A granita is like an Italian ice, but coarser and quite grainy in texture, hence its name. It makes a refreshing dessert after a rich main course, or a cooling treat on a hot summer's day.

Serves 6

INGREDIENTS
4 large oranges
1 large lemon
¾ cup granulated sugar
2 cups water
amaretti cookies, to serve

oranges *sugar*

amaretti cookies

lemon

1 Thinly pare the zest from the oranges and lemon, trying to avoid the bitter white pith, and set a few pieces aside for decoration. Halve the fruit and squeeze the juice into a pitcher. Set aside.

COOK'S TIP
To make the decoration, slice the orange and lemon zest into thin strips. Blanch for 2 minutes, refresh under cold water and dry before using.

2 Heat the sugar and water in a heavy saucepan, stirring over low heat, until the sugar dissolves. Bring to a boil, then boil without stirring for about 10 minutes, until a syrup forms. Remove the syrup from the heat, add the orange and lemon zest and shake the pan. Cover and let cool.

3 Strain the sugar syrup into a shallow freezer container and add the fruit juice. Stir well to mix, then freeze, uncovered, for about 4 hours, until slushy.

4 Take the half-frozen mixture from the freezer and mix with a fork. Freeze for 4 more hours, or until hard. To serve, let sit at room temperature for about 10 minutes, then break up with a fork and pile into long-stemmed glasses. Decorate with strips of zest (see Cook's Tip) and serve with amaretti cookies.

Tiramisù

The name of this popular dessert translates as "pick me up," which is said to derive from the fact that it is so good that it literally makes you swoon when you eat it. There are many, many versions, and the recipe can be adapted to suit your own taste—you can vary the amounts of the ingredients, or make it in individual serving dishes, if desired.

Serves 6–8

INGREDIENTS

3 eggs, separated
2 cups mascarpone cheese, at room
    temperature
1 teaspoon vanilla sugar
¾ cup cold, very strong black coffee
½ cup Kahlua or other coffee-
    flavored liqueur
18 savoiardi (Italian sponge fingers)
sifted unsweetened cocoa powder
    and grated bittersweet chocolate,
    to finish

vanilla sugar

eggs

cocoa powder

bittersweet chocolate

mascarpone cheese

coffee-flavored liqueur

savoiardi

coffee powder

1 Put the egg whites in a grease-free bowl and beat with an electric mixer until stiff and in peaks.

2 Mix the mascarpone, vanilla sugar and egg yolks in a separate large bowl and beat with the electric mixer until evenly combined. Fold in the egg whites. Spread a few spoonfuls of the mixture in the bottom of a large serving bowl.

3 Combine the coffee and liqueur in a shallow dish. Dip a sponge finger in the mixture, turn it quickly so that it becomes saturated but does not disintegrate, and place it on top of the mascarpone mixture in the bowl. Add five more dipped sponge fingers, placing them side by side.

4 Spoon in about one-third of the remaining mascarpone mixture and spread it out. Make more layers in the same way, ending with mascarpone. Level the surface, then sift cocoa powder over it. Cover and chill overnight. Before serving, sprinkle with more cocoa and the grated chocolate.

Ricotta Cheesecake

Low-fat ricotta cheese is excellent for cheesecake
fillings because it creates a good, firm texture.
Here it is enriched with eggs and cream and
enlivened with tangy orange and lemon zest to
make a Sicilian-style dessert.

Serves 8

INGREDIENTS
16 ounces (2 cups) low-fat
   ricotta cheese
½ cup heavy cream
2 eggs
1 egg yolk
⅓ cup granulated sugar
finely grated zest of 1 orange
finely grated zest of 1 lemon
blanched thin strips of orange and
   lemon zest, to decorate

FOR THE PASTRY
1½ cups all-purpose flour
3 tablespoons granulated sugar
pinch of salt
8 tablespoons (1 stick) chilled
   butter, diced
1 egg yolk

heavy cream

ricotta cheese

sugar   *flour*

eggs   *orange*

butter   *lemon*

1 Make the pastry. Sift the flour, sugar
and salt onto a cold work surface. Make
a well in the center and put in the diced
butter and egg yolk. Gradually work the
flour into the diced butter and egg yolk,
using your fingertips.

2 Gather the dough together, reserve
about a quarter for the lattice, then press
the rest into a 9-inch fluted tart pan with
a removable bottom. Chill the pastry
shell for 30 minutes.

3 Meanwhile, preheat the oven to
375°F and make the filling. Put the
ricotta, cream, eggs, egg yolk, sugar and
grated orange and lemon zests in a large
bowl and beat until the ingredients are
evenly mixed.

4 Prick the bottom of the pastry shell,
then line with foil and fill with baking
beans, raw rice or pastry weights. Bake
blind for 15 minutes, then transfer to a
wire rack, remove the foil and beans and
let the pastry shell cool in the pan.

5 Spoon the cheese and cream filling
into the pastry shell and level the surface.
Roll out the reserved dough and cut into
strips. Arrange the strips on top of the
filling in a lattice pattern, sticking them in
place with water.

6 Bake the cheesecake for
30–35 minutes, until golden and set.
Transfer to a wire rack and let cool
thoroughly, then carefully remove the
side of the pan and slide the
cheesecake onto a serving plate.
Decorate with blanched thin strips of
orange and lemon zest before serving.

VARIATIONS
Add ⅓–⅔ cup finely chopped
candied peel to the filling in
step 3, or ⅓ cup semisweet
chocolate chips.
   For a really rich dessert, you can
add both candied peel and some
grated semisweet chocolate.

Zabaglione

A much-loved, simple Italian pudding traditionally made with Marsala, an Italian fortified wine. Madeira is a good alternative.

Serves 4

INGREDIENTS
4 egg yolks
¼ cup granulated sugar
¼ cup Marsala or Madeira wine
amaretti cookies, to serve

eggs

sugar

Marsala

amaretti cookies

1 Place the egg yolks and sugar in a large, clean heatproof bowl and beat with an electric mixer until the mixture is pale and thick and forms fluffy peaks when the beaters are lifted out of the egg mixture.

2 Gradually add the Marsala, beating well after each addition (at this stage the mixture will be quite runny).

3 Now place over a pan of gently simmering water and continue to beat for 5–7 minutes, until the mixture becomes thick and mousse-like; when the beaters are lifted, they should leave a thick trail on the surface of the mixture.

4 Pour into four warmed stemmed glasses and serve immediately, with the amaretti cookies for dipping.

COOK'S TIP
Make sure the zabaglione is thick and mousse-like; if you don't beat the mixture for long enough, the zabaglione will be too runny and will probably separate.

VARIATION
If you don't have any Marsala or Madeira, you could use a medium-sweet sherry or a dessert wine.

Stuffed Peaches with Mascarpone Cream

Mascarpone is a thick, velvety Italian cream cheese, made from cow's milk. It is often used in desserts, or eaten with fresh fruit.

Serves 4

INGREDIENTS
4 large peaches, halved and pitted
¾ cup amaretti cookie crumbs
2 tablespoons ground almonds
3 tablespoons granulated sugar
1 tablespoon unsweetened
    cocoa powder
⅔ cup sweet wine
2 tablespoons butter

FOR THE MASCARPONE CREAM
2 tablespoons superfine sugar
3 egg yolks
1 tablespoon sweet wine
1 cup mascarpone cheese
⅔ cup heavy cream

1 Preheat the oven to 400°F. Using a teaspoon, scoop some of the flesh from the cavities in the peaches to make a reasonable space for stuffing. Chop the scooped-out flesh.

peaches *ground almonds* *butter* *amaretti cookies* *mascarpone cheese* *superfine sugar* *sugar* *heavy cream* *eggs* *sweet wine* *cocoa powder*

2 Combine the amaretti cookies, ground almonds, sugar, cocoa and peach flesh in a bowl. Add enough wine to make the mixture into a thick paste. Place the peaches in a buttered ovenproof dish and fill them with the amaretti and almond stuffing. Dot with butter, then pour the remaining wine into the dish. Bake for 35 minutes.

3 To make the mascarpone cream, beat the sugar and egg yolks until thick and pale. Stir in the wine, then fold in the mascarpone. Whip the cream until it forms soft peaks and fold into the mixture. Remove the peaches from the oven and let cool. Serve the peaches at room temperature, with the mascarpone cream.

INDEX